RECONCILED

True Stories and Insights to Mending Broken Relationships

PORTIA L. HEWITT

DEDICATION

Jesus Christ
This book is dedicated to my Lord and Saviour Jesus Christ who gave His life to reconcile me.

My Family
To my loving husband, Joseph, with whom I have shared 35 years of marriage. Together we have learned the importance of commitment, unconditional love, and saying I'm sorry. You are my friend, my brother in Christ, my spouse, and my pastor! I am forever grateful for your ministry, which has greatly contributed to my understanding of reconciliation. I love you more than you know and feel honored to walk out this great salvation by your side. To my children, Jared & Rachel, you bring so much encouragement and joy to my life! This world is a better place because you two are in it. To Mother, thank you for your love and wisdom, and for being an example of the Proverbs 31 woman. To my sisters Angela and Glenda, you have always been my cheerleaders and for that I am forever grateful.

Special People
To the courageous women who willingly shared their stories, may you be richly blessed because you stepped forward to bless others.

To my friend Angela Wynn who encouraged me to pursue my dream by pursuing hers.

To the women of Reconciliation Word Ministry International whose love and prayers helped me get across the finish line!

In Loving Memory
To my dad, A.T. Thomas who taught me the importance of
excellence and making a difference. To my sister Alecia, a woman
of many artistic talents and infectious laughter—rest on. I love and
miss you both.

All Scripture References are from the King James Version of the
Holy Bible.

A Special Note:
The true stories contained in this book were voluntarily written
and voluntarily submitted: they are used by permission. In certain
cases, names and locations have been changed to protect and
honor parties involved.

Book Cover Design by Apollonia P. Middlebrooks

ISBN: 978-1-7362420-1-8

Contents

FOREWORD

The adversary would like nothing more than to enact his opposition with God in our earthly relationships—to set this one against that one, using inevitable hurts and challenges we face in this life. To be unaware of this subtle device, is to risk never experiencing the transformative power of reconciliation. For this reason, reconciliation is a personal chapter that, for many of us, remains unwritten.

Patently, the issues of life often bring us to places of hurt and unforgiveness. The mere thought of reconciling with those who have hurt us, tends to frustrate our personal philosophies about fairness and retribution. Even if we are open to the process, the path toward reconciliation is often one of uncertainty, discomfort, and/or resistance. This is especially true if the person with whom we are unreconciled is deceased. Often times we are instructed to *forgive* or *let go*, without corresponding guidance on how to apply that directive.

This book is a unique gift in that it provides real-life examples of reconciliation put into faith-based action. Through the illustrative accounts of several women of faith, and from a biblical viewpoint on the matter, Lady Portia Hewitt deepens our understanding of reconciliation and identifies the key components central to its process. The reader is taken on a journey from enmity with the very concept of reconciliation squarely to the foot of the cross, where our reconciliation story truly begins. This book is much more than an entertaining read or a conversational piece for social soirees—it is a paradigm shift. Having known Lady Portia for many years as an anointed teacher and loving spiritual mother, her prompting of paradigm shifts comes as no surprise. Through the word and love of God, she emboldens women to adopt a Godly self-view in order to foster their transformation from stale story to living epistle.

Although movement occurs whether we are sifted by our adversary or shifted by our Advocate, the gravity of those outcomes are vastly different. My prayer for the reader is that a shift occurs while reading this book, one that involves moving from mere human reasoning to spiritual revelation. With that said, I'm grateful that my own assumptions about the impossibility of reconciliation (based on type of hurt) were challenged and laid aside while reading this book. In exchange, I walked away with this very truth: our Advocate, Jesus Christ, would like nothing more than to demonstrate His reconciliation story within *every* facet of my life—to convert those relational hurts and challenges into testimonies of liberation. To align with His sovereign design—even when it seems impossible—is to position myself to both experience and minister the transformative power of reconciliation. For this purpose, reconciliation will become a personal chapter that I will finally begin to write.

May you be transformed and equipped by the reading of this book.

Keisha Bell, PhD, Clinical Psychologist

PREFACE

Reconciliation is a six-syllable word that few people mention short of managing their checkbook or reversing the pitfalls of divorce. But the word reconciliation means something more relevant and life-impacting; it's a state that speaks to an active re-engagement of broken relationships. Reconciliation is such an intrinsic part of everyday life that most people are not cognizant when it's at work.

Reconciliation is about everyday life and everyday living and is ever active and ever achievable being a significant entity in the lives of people of every tongue, tribe, and nation. Genderless, ageless, and race-less, reconciliation is about people resolving issues, healing wounds, and even changing the course of broken relationships. Just considering reconciling ignites hope of harmony and peaceful coexistence between family or friends. People dream, "If only she hadn't done that, we would still be together!" Or they ponder, "Would we still be married if I only …." Reconciliation cannot change the past, but it's certainly the answer to achieving a new, harmonious future. And that alone must become the central focus. Anything that hinders the process is nothing more than a minor hurdle. That includes memories of mistrust, misunderstanding, betrayal, and yes, even the pain of grief and loss experienced when meaningful relationships cease. These memories alone cause many to halt the process, concluding: "I can't do it!" "I won't do it!" Or, "It's not worth it!" And so for some the undertaking often ends before beginning.

What is Reconciliation: an act or state of an active process that brings hostile persons or those experiencing discord back into a harmonious, agreeable situation. Reconciliation includes resolving quarrels, and winning individuals back into friendliness, making the incompatible compatible, and putting an end to the opposition. With so many apparent benefits, however, many people still find reconciling fearsome and daunting. Becoming harmonious with others means revealing oneself and likewise accepting others as they are — naked realities that can be unsettling. Why? Presenting "the real me," could cause people to reject me.

Preeminent questions:
- Is the relationship worth saving?
- Does this person add to the quality of my life, or do they drain it?
- Can I look past what happened and do whatever it takes to restore the relationship?
- What will make it right again?
- Is there anything worth salvaging?
- Am I prepared to walk away if they reject me?

Be candid in weighing the options: (a) should I put shortcomings aside and become an agent to reconcile or (b) should I become the catalyst to sever ties for good? Hard questions, hard choices.

Reconciliation is about a reunion, beginning again, and moving past discord to establish true harmony. It requires communication and commitment, coexisting in enjoyable times, and times of adversity. Reconciliation requires change in attitude, behavior, and dialogue to avoid the pitfalls of disunity and strife once experienced. What are the two most important factors that facilitate reconciliation: forgiveness, and renewed vision.

One of the most ardent enemies of reunification is having the attitude, "I forgive you, but I will never forget what you did!" Another is looking for old attitudes, behaviors, and failures—expecting the other person to repeat whatever caused the break up. For true reconciliation to occur, you must extend unconditional forgiveness and envision change in the other person. Don't look for things to be the way they were. Expect better! Forge a new path and expect others to do the same. Remember—it's worth it to fight for significant relationships with people you love!

In a random survey, I asked people, *"Why do you think some people are not willing to reconcile with others?"* Here are just a few candid responses:

"Fear of Rejection"
"One of the reasons that I believe that some are not willing to reconcile with others is fear of rejection. The person may feel that what happened was too devastating to ignore. I've reached out to my family member, hoping to begin work on mending our estranged relationship and never received a response. I don't want to think that I'm being rejected or ignored. Perhaps they're just not ready to respond to me."
S.A.

"Lack of forgiveness and Pride."

"I believe some people are not willing to reconcile with people for two reasons: unforgiveness and pride. Many people suffer from pain and rejection from conflict amongst one another. Due to these feelings, an individual may harbor ill feelings that prevent them from healing. Then pride can set in, hindering the pursuit of peace. As a result, some have carried ancestral pain throughout generations."

K.H.

"Fear"

"Some people let fear override their desire to be obedient and step out on faith."

A.B.

"Physical and Mental Health"

"Perhaps they feel better not being around an unlikable or even 'toxic' person. You can love someone with the love of the Lord and still not like his or her ways. Tough love precludes reconciliation...for some time, at least."

A.G.

"The Pain Outweighs the Urgency to Forgive"

"I think some people are not willing to reconcile with others because they feel that the depth of their hurt, pain, or shame is too bad to allow them to forgive or reconcile with the other person. But what they fail to realize is that Jesus Christ suffered every type of pain, humiliation, disappointment, betrayal, and ridicule imaginable to cleanse us from our sins. Because God has forgiven us of our sins so we should be willing to forgive others."

J.T.

With these responses, it is easy to see that forgiving is at the forefront in patching up broken relationships. But how many of us understand what it means to forgive? I've often heard people say, "I will forgive her, but I won't forget what she did!" Or something like, "If I forgive her, does that mean I have to make her my friend?" And better yet, "I forgive her, but I don't trust her!" These are valid concerns for considering the possibility of redeeming a lost relationship.

Forgive & Forget

Our most perfect state as human beings is when we are children—innocent. A child can suffer abuse from his parent and still cling to them with all their might. He can have a drag down fight with a classmate at recess and be friends again by dismissal. Why? Because unforgiveness is not natural—we learn it. Two critical words, "I'm sorry," do make everything right in the eyes of a child.

Throughout the typical life, reconciliation will become necessary at almost every age and stage of development and in every relationship. Little girls will forgive each other for arguments experienced at playdates. Boys will overcome conflict and exercise good sportsmanship no matter how they hoop or tackle. Teen girls will forgive their moms for strict rules, and moms will forgive their daughters for breaking them. Spouses will argue, kiss, and makeup. All these are examples of reconciliation.

On the flip side of what happens in everyday life, are those not-too-common impossible situations that require a miracle. Like rejoining individuals who suffered violence, betrayal, or mental or sexual abuse. These, the toughest of circumstances, could warrant total and complete physical separation, leaving even the most ardent optimist with diminishing hopes of seeing meaningful relationships mended.

Reconciliation is a six-syllable concept described by several three-syllable words: together, compromise, agreement, congruence, harmony, and unity. It is a word that summarizes restoring, reuniting, and yes, resuming a broken relationship. But if we take the time to analyze reconciliation, we would realize that without it, marriages would cease to exist. Families all over the world would be fragmented. Friendships would be short-lived. And not too many people would have the testimony of having longstanding and meaningful relationships.

This work examines the significance, necessity, and components of reconciliation. Most importantly, it shows the miracle of God's hand that makes reunion possible. It will illustrate, through personal testimony, the journey of several women who weathered storms of betrayal, hurt, and brokenness, to experience forgiveness—how they found harmony, love, and joy again in relationships made new by God.

I am sincerely grateful to the sisters who joined me on this liberating journey. They are senior citizens, college graduates, daughters, and mothers—women of various ages who disclosed their painful experiences that others might be made whole and inspired to recover lost, meaningful relationships. I am also grateful to my God, who moved upon my husband-pastor to rename the church, Reconciliation Word Ministry, International. The change necessitated that we revise our mission, and re-engage believers to become active reconcilers according to 2 Corinthians 5:19.

"To wit, that God was in Christ, reconciling the world unto himself, not imputing their trespasses unto them; and hath committed unto us the word of reconciliation."

This verse reveals that we have a crucial assignment: to reconcile souls to Christ. But before we can do that, our walk must show evidence of a reconciled lifestyle—both to Christ and to other people. This work presents that evidence.

INTRODUCTION

Life is a Journey

Literary buffs and historians know that it was Ralph Waldo Emerson who declared, "Life is a journey." But what he said was, "Life is a journey, not a destination." So often we gather up our things, get dressed up, pick up our keys, and head for the train station—assuming that everything will be all right when we get "there." Then somewhere along the journey, we come to realize "There" is somewhere we strive to go for our entire lives. When do we arrive at that place called "There?"

I'm sure I was well out of my 20's when I realized that I was missing out on so many meaningful experiences along the journey to the ultimate destination. Thinking, "I'll address it when I get there." Now, I'm preparing to take my first proper road trip, and I realize that my entire life has been one big road trip. I've learned to pack for quick flights, extended family vacations, and one-day trips. Each time I met unfamiliar people, saw different places and had unexpected conversations. I found that I was more affected by the people I met along the way than I cared to admit. There were also times that I regretted meeting certain people. Some experiences were pleasant. Some were not. But in retrospect, I can say that every encounter added meaning, revelation, and even relevance to my life. I have grown through every experience. This journey, with all its twists and unexpected turns, has also birthed in me fresh hope that when people interact with people, astonishing things happen.

1

Every positive encounter reminded me that there are plenty of loving people in this world. People with sincere hope fueled by fervent prayers and a desire to be all God intends. The negative encounters, however, served as a reminder of my shortcomings. I realized that I was not above losing my temper or making wrong assumptions; that I was more fragile than I should be; and that I should never be above making or receiving an apology. But they also reminded me of the prevailing sin that rules in the hearts of so many. Some people hurt others for personal gain. Not everyone rejoices when you receive a promotion or blessing. They would rather spit on your congratulations card, sabotage your wedding, and even worse, call your bank to demand they cancel your car loan because they couldn't get one. People rejoice with you, but some are envious of you. This knowledge compelled me to look at the balances of life. I juxtaposed the philanthropists who spend their lives and substance meeting other's needs versus those filled with greed who prey on the misfortunate to supply their coffers. I assessed every encounter, the good, the bad, the pleasant, and the painful. I found that each one has contributed to my journey as I traverse through life to that place called "there."

Every encounter with an optimist adds a brighter perspective to an otherwise dull day. Some people just seem to see the "sunny side" of life no matter what. These optimists have found the secret to keeping their focus on the good. They enjoy life, it's prospects, and every opportunity presented. That's one reason adults

2

love being around small children. Interacting with a child can rekindle the hope of a world filled with new joy, sincerity, and innocence.

Conversing with an older adult highlights the essential qualities of wisdom and tenacity through the good and the bad: life is brief and, it's imperative to make every minute count, and every relationship cherished. It's all about balance. People of every age and walk of life can add fresh perspectives conducive to forming a positive outlook. My gratitude factor elevates when I consider other's misfortunes. Meeting the underprivileged is the best reminder that things aren't as bad as they could get. They help us appreciate our blessings and to be thankful for even the bare necessities of food and sustenance. Meeting and interacting with others can enliven new perspectives, wisdom, and introspection. It can present endless opportunities to receive and even more occasions to give.

Navigating your way through life is akin to plotting your course on a map. "You are here," are three revealing words that mark the starting point of every journey. Before you can plot out the course for getting "there," you must concede to the revelation: "You are here." Until you face your "here," you cannot begin your trek to that place called "there."

The reality of "here," however, can be painful to ponder when thoughts flash back to the road traveled to get "here." What circumstances brought me here? Who was involved in my journey? What did I do that caused me to be in this place? Is it my fault? Whose fault is it? The latter two questions so often seem to take preeminence over all others. What matters most is "Where do I go from here?"

No one can argue the relevance the past plays in plotting the course of the future. Spending too much time looking back can hinder the impetus to forge ahead. History is important, but gaining momentum to move forward into the future is most important! Let's face it—looking back for too long can do more damage than good. I once heard my pastor illustrate this point using the constructs of a car; the front windshield is vast and wide to help you see where you are going. But the rear-view mirror is only a fraction of its size. You need to be aware of what's behind you, but you need to cast your vision on what is ahead of you! Take a brief look back. But steady your view on what's ahead. Otherwise, you will crash!

The stories in Reconciled disclose experiences from courageous women who dared to look back long enough to inspire others to move forward!

The accounts you are about to read are true. They contain meaningful descriptions, definitions, facts, and even poetry that herald the heart of emotions evoked when relationships end. The authors gladly contributed their reconciliation encounters hoping that every reader would take a bold leap to heal brokenness in their own lives. Everyone has a story. But not everyone recognizes the lasting effects people and situations impose as they journey through life's stages. I am grateful to the women who relived their pain, tears, and struggles to create a purposeful template for others. May you find hope, healing, and help to pursue and recover significant relationships in your life.

God's Boundless Mercy
Sallie's Story

Sometimes one may wonder, LORD, why was I even born? Am I a member of this family or just a facsimile of Cinderella with a familiar last name? My story tells how God's boundless mercy kept me throughout my childhood and until this very moment.

At seventeen, my mother married my biological father, Theo T. He walked away, leaving my mother with a 16-month-old daughter, just two months before I was born. She said she thought if she jumped from the top steps of the porch, that second baby would come earlier. She said she didn't know what else to do. I was born a very healthy baby and, given the name Sarah. When my older sister Joyce was four years old, and I was three years old, my mother married our stepfather Lester G.

My mother and my stepfather moved away from Wellspring to Mobile, Alabama. He treated us kindly, allowing us to call him Daddy, and he loved my mother. We believed that he loved us too. We lived like any other average family. Attending Antioch Baptist Church, and we were very active members. I loved the church, so I was always there and reading my Bible. When I was about ten years old, the LORD gave me specific chapters to read. As HE opened my understanding, He became more real, more alive to me. Every time I was in His presence, I could do nothing but

7

cry and tell HIM how much I loved HIM. Daddy said to me I would have to stop reading the Bible, or I would end up in the crazy house. Momma agreed with him, so they took away my Bible.

During this time, my mother became pregnant with my sister Nadine. Nadine was a very beautiful little baby. Joyce worked after school at Mr. Timber's candy store, so I had to do my chores plus some of hers. I also had to take care of Nadine. That was hard. But one good thing—I got my Bible back! Unfortunately, I was so tired that I couldn't read as much as I wanted to. After Nadine was born, Momma had seven more children, three born in Alabama, and four born in Ohio.

One day, during my mother's third pregnancy Joyce went to the outhouse. That's when it happened. My stepfather did something unmentionable to her. But Joyce did what many girls don't have the courage to do; she told, but Momma didn't believe her. She sided with her husband. I wasn't there that day. At the time, I was at church, rehearsing for an upcoming play.

When I got home, I saw Joyce tied to a kitchen chair, and Daddy was beating her with an extension cord for telling lies. The very man who had raised her as his own daughter was beating her. The same man who violated her. She was fifteen when it happened.

Joyce's escape came through marrying a very nice older man that year. It was the same year she would have started ninth grade. She never completed high school. Now, she has mental issues. She refuses to admit that anything this awful could ever happen.

When I turned 15, we moved to Ohio. My stepfather provided well for us. He had always worked at manufacturing companies—when we moved, he had positions at two companies. It was almost two years later when I was seventeen. Momma went to the hospital after Maelyn was born. As the oldest, I took care of the younger children, because Daddy had to work. It was more difficult this time because I noticed that my stepfather was drinking more. That Friday, he was frying fish. He did all the cooking. The kids were in their room playing, and he called me to come into the kitchen. I went to see what he wanted. He told me to kiss him. I told him no. The more I said no, the more demanding he was. It was raining very hard that day, and as the raindrops fell to the earth, I remembered that day when he beat my sister for telling Momma what he did to her. He was so angry with me. I dared not let him know how afraid I was of him. "No!" It would not happen to me. And it did not—because that day, the day I said no, he put me out. I had no money, I had no clothes, and I had nowhere to go.

Reflection

What happens when life itself feels like an enemy? When the very system created to educate, nurture and train, instead becomes an asylum of hostility, devastation, and uncertainty; when the young quickly acquaints with the old, losing the shelter of their innocence. What happens when severing of relationship becomes the only alternative to safety and survival. Can this be reconciled?

Child abuse is a malady that devastates children around the globe, leaving them with emotional and relational problems that can follow them throughout their lives. And talking with victims, young and old, they describe the after-effects as including any of the following feelings: isolation, shame, anger, and guilt. Working in ministry for over twenty years, I met children who were so scarred and abused that they were angry with God, their families, and the world. With their slashed arms, they lashed out to beat down anyone who came near them at school, at church, or at home. I met young women who felt raped by the husbands who vowed to love them, and teens that engaged in uncontrollable promiscuity because exploring these behaviors had become an unwelcome part of their lives soon after they learned to tie their shoes. In social service, I met little boys who had been left in the care of known sex offenders and girls with blank stares who refused to be loved. Victims. They are everywhere.

Sallie's Story Continued

LORD, why was I born? My mother jumped from a high place, trying to force an early birth that I might die. I guess it was an act of desperation. My sister, my friend, my protector, left me. She got married and moved to

Wyoming. After she left, the family disregarded me. They never invited me to family outings. I was always told: "there is not enough room for you. Maybe next time."

"And David said unto Gad, I am in a great strait: let us fall now into the hand of the LORD; for his mercies are great: and let me not fall into the hand of man." (2 Samuel 24:14)

I walked to the bus stop, and I stood there with tears streaming from my eyes. A man came out of his workplace and saw me crying, my clothing soaking wet from the rain. He asked why I was out in this weather without wearing proper clothing. I told him that I had no place to go, and that my father put me out of his house, and my mother was in the hospital. He suggested that I stay with a friend until Momma came home. I remembered Momma's friend Miss Ida Belle. I told him that she lived on the westside of town and I should be able to stay overnight at her house. He gave me enough bus fare to get to her house. I asked the LORD to please let her be home when I arrived. He heard my prayer. I told her what happened, and she welcomed me into her home, along with her three daughters. I found a job babysitting. And because I supported myself, I was not able to return to school. Miss Ida Belle received General assistance for herself and her children. Until I found a job, she shared what she had with me. It was an on-time favor when I needed it most.

"Surely goodness and mercy shall follow me all the days of my life…" (Psalm 23:6)

Component of Reconciliation: Love

Reflection

A famous songwriter penned the words, "What the world needs now is love, sweet love." And he was so right. His song expounded on so many plenteous things in the world; cornfields, wheat fields, even mountains. But the one thing that seemed in short supply—love. What this songwriter didn't mention, though, was how to get it!

Everyone wants love. Dogs wag their tails when they detect it. Couples rejoice when they find it. But children—they thrive when they receive love. I have had several conversations with men, women, and even children who confessed that their parents never told them, "I love you!"

In most cases, it left the children growing up wondering if they were lovable. They felt naked, unsure even broken-hearted well into their adult years. Some moved forward in life, vowing to shower their children with love. But others had difficulty forming lasting relationships, drifting from person to person, or marriage to marriage. They found themselves unable to connect, even with their own children.

People frequently talk about showing love. But few explain how to do it. The problem is many think love is a feeling—something warm and fuzzy, gooey, and emotional. The problem with this perspective is that when you don't "feel the feeling," does that mean you cannot or should not emit the actions of love? Is giving love optional? Are there conditions under which acts of love are not suitable?

What is love?

Love is a spirit. 1John 4:8 unveils the exact origin of love: "God is love." John 4:24 reveals: "God is a Spirit." Putting these two verses together, we can conclude that Love Is A Spirit. And therefore acting in the Spirit of Love, we can, with pure conscience, treat people lovingly, even when we don't feel it.

What is the Behavior of Love?

The epistle writer Paul best answers this question in his epistle to the Christians at Corinth, however the word he used—charity.

1 Corinthians 13:1-8
Though I speak with the tongues of men and of angels, and have not charity, I am become as sounding brass, or a tinkling cymbal. And though I have the gift of prophecy, and understand all mysteries, and all knowledge; and though I have all faith, so that I could remove mountains, and have not charity, I am nothing. And though I bestow all my goods to feed the poor, and though I give my body to be burned, and have not charity, it profiteth me nothing. Charity suffereth long, and is kind; charity envieth not; charity vaunteth not itself, is not puffed up, Doth not behave itself unseemly, seeketh not her own, is not

easily provoked, thinketh no evil; Rejoiceth not in iniquity, but rejoiceth in the truth; Beareth all things, believeth all things, hopeth all things, endureth all things. Charity never faileth: but whether there be prophecies, they shall fail; whether there be tongues, they shall cease; whether there be knowledge, it shall vanish away.

Put simply—love in action is never about me; love is all about you! Genuine love propels a person to care deeply about another, with unfailing patience, kindness, faith, endurance, and hope. Active love blesses others, which results in pure joy. It always thinks the best of a person, giving the benefit of the doubt in situations. Love is not relative to conditions, decisions, or actions. It is not contingent or conditional. Love is the one constant that never changes—even when people change. Genuine love is always there, giving, expecting nothing in return.

How many people have experienced that kind of love? How many children know that even when they get poor grades, their parents will still love them? Or when they get into trouble, they will receive an outstretched hand to rescue them from their fallen state? And what about people that have disagreements—do they know that the love between them can condition the atmosphere for productive communication where they can find agreement?

When there is genuine love, there is true charity.

I wrote my mother a letter, and I apologized to her for leaving as I did. I did not want yet another daughter to hurt her, accusing her husband of incestuous rape. So I just asked her to please forgive me. The lie I told—that the children had just become too much for me—seemed like the most straightforward explanation to escape without severing our relationship or hurting her.

One day after an outing, when I returned to the place I called home, to my surprise, my mother was sitting in Miss Ida Belle's living room. I was petrified. I thought, "I am about to undergo the same suffering as Joyce." I had already talked to a pastor who told me to keep it to myself "because no one should interfere in a marriage."

My mother asked me to sit down beside her on the couch. I sat by her, and she took my hand, looked me in my eyes and talked to me:

"I want you to tell me the truth. You don't have to be afraid, I have made many mistakes in my life, and I need to correct as many of them as possible. I have already talked to Joyce, and she will be here this summer. And I know that you are the most honorable of all my children, Sarah. You are special. You think I don't love you, but I do. Your father has done many wrong things during the time we have been married. Tell me the truth what did he do to you?"

15

It was time to deal with this, and I was so ready to talk to her.

"He did nothing Momma, He was drinking, and insisted that I do things that were very sinful in the eyes of GOD, and I would not do them. He got mad and threw me out of the house during the storm." That day I knew she heard me—even believed me. Momma apologized for him, but he never said he was sorry. Not until the day he was making his transition. And I said to him, "Daddy, I forgave you when I first stepped through the doors years ago. You just needed to forgive yourself. Joyce has forgiven you too." He closed his eyes and fell asleep to wait for the only judgment that mattered.

I was very young when I experienced that storm and didn't know too much about prayer, what to pray for, or even if God would hear me. I thought no one cared about me, other than having me do their chores. Miss Ida Belle was always telling me that Momma loved me and that she missed me. But in reality, not one day of my life could I remember my mother saying, "I love you." I didn't think Momma cared enough to even check on me until she showed up at Miss Ida's house. That day I learned that Miss Ida Bell and her next-door neighbor had been keeping my mother informed about how I was getting along.

The encounter between my mother and me was a complete surprise. Momma said that she had always loved me, and Joyce too, but she never knew how to tell us because when she was growing up, no one told her, "I love you." Momma still could not embrace me, but she did hold my hand. It was a beginning. Upon this single encounter, we would build the foundation of our mother-daughter relationship. It would take years, but at least I had hope for what always seemed so far away, even impossible: I would have a relationship with my mother.

LORD GOD, I thank you. Your Boundless Mercy has been my refuge through the wounds I experienced from my mother and my father. Your loving kindness surrounds me. I praise you, Jesus, *"For thy mercy is great above the heavens: and thy truth reacheth unto the clouds."* *(Psalms 108:4)* Father, you are my only stronghold, and you only can bring together my broken pieces. I bless you, Lord.

"Thou wilt shew me the path of life: in thy presence is fulness of joy; at thy right hand there are pleasures forevermore." *(Psalms 16:11)*

Reflection

Not every reconciliation story will end in the manner we expect. That's the bad news. The good news is that though you suffered when the relationship became fractured, through prayer and faith, you will experience relief through mending what seemed lost forever. Through this process, you will gain courage, strength, comfort, and confidence to complete your reconciliation journey. And as in Sallie's case, you may be surprised by what you learn. It must have been devastating to grow up in a house with no hugs—not one declaration of, "I love you." But it is just as painful to learn that your mother also grew up the same way. Such knowledge can transform pain into empathy for another.

Reconciliation makes room for compassion.
Reconciliation requires you to forgive.

Component of Reconciliation: Forgiveness—Cancel the Debt!

Isn't it amazing that reconciliatory activities sound more like financial business ventures? Most people understand this process to be a method of checks and balances— ensuring that your personal ledger matches your bank statement. To reconcile the account is to verify that records reveal a consistent and harmonious account of monies received and monies spent. The basic premise, therefore, is the agreement between two records. When more money goes out than comes in, this creates liability or debt. That means owing something. But dictionaries also define the word debt as meaning sin. Finally, after weeding through countless banking and debt sites, I found what I searched for—issues concerning the human heart. Jesus addressed the concept of debt in a profound parable:

Matthew 18:21-35

"Then came Peter to him, and said, Lord, how oft shall my brother sin against me, and I forgive him? till seven times? Jesus saith unto him, I say not unto thee, Until seven times: but, Until seventy times seven. Therefore is the kingdom of heaven likened unto a certain king, which would take account of his servants. And when he had begun to reckon, one was brought unto him, which owed him ten thousand talents. But forasmuch as he had not to pay, his lord commanded him to be sold, and his wife, and children, and all that he had, and payment to be made. The servant therefore fell down, and worshipped him, saying, Lord, have patience with me, and I will pay thee all. Then the lord of that servant was moved with compassion, and loosed him, and forgave him the debt. But the same servant went out, and found one of his fellowservants, which owed him an hundred pence: and he laid hands on him, and took him by the throat, saying, Pay me that thou owest. And his fellowservant fell down at his feet, and besought him, saying, Have patience with me, and I will pay thee all. And he would not: but went and cast him into prison, till he should pay the debt. So when his fellowservants saw what was done, they were very sorry, and came and told unto their lord all that was done. Then his lord, after that he had called him, said unto him, O thou wicked servant, I forgave thee all that debt, because thou desiredst me: Shouldest not thou also have had compassion on thy fellowservant, even as I had pity on thee? And his lord was wroth, and delivered him to the tormentors, till he should pay all that was due unto him. So likewise shall my heavenly Father do also unto you, if ye from your hearts forgive not every one his brother their trespasses."

This parable beautifully illustrates both financial and spiritual debt, but most importantly, "debt cancellation." Rather than calling the debt, which was large enough for the entire family to be sold for the payoff, the compassionate lord released his servant from a debt equivalent to $150,000.00! The word for such generosity is charity, which scholars define as "impartial love."

What would your reaction be if your mortgage lender called to inform you that they cancelled your house note, and you could just live there for free—unbelief, joy, relief? Undoubtedly, the greatest of emotions should be thankfulness! And in the famous words of Christ, "Freely ye have received, freely give" (Matthew 10:8). This simple clause reveals the expected attitude of one who has received—give! The parable, however, does not end there. It continues: the same servant who was forgiven so much had lent 100 pence to another. That amount translates to about 100 pennies! When he played the role of the debtor, however, he was not so merciful. He not only insisted that the pennies be repaid, but he threw the borrower into prison until he was able to pay! When the charitable lord heard this story, greatly angered, he reversed the kindness he extended to the unmerciful lord, seeing his actions as undeniable evidence of his ungrateful heart.

This parable illustrates a life-changing principle; those whose debts get cancelled, should cancel debts owed to them. Those forgiven should in kind, forgive.

Being wronged by someone who says they love you can sever a relationship. The question is, "if you love me, how can you hurt me?" Yet another question: "if you love me, why can't you forgive me? Love and forgiveness go hand-in-hand. Even in the best of relationships, someone will offend another. The question is: will the offended be able to forgive? And if so, how many times? Once? Twice? I have often heard people say, "Three times, and you're out!" But relationships are not ball games. If they were, people would never get to home base! Just look at what Jesus said about forgiveness:

"Then came Peter to him, and said, Lord, how oft shall my brother sin against me, and I forgive him? till seven times? Jesus saith unto him, I say not unto thee, Until seven times: but, Until seventy times seven" (Matthew 18:21-22).

Take the limits off!

Where sin abounded, grace did much more abound
(Romans 5:20)

Paul's insights shed incredible light on the hard question: how many times should we forgive? Can we apply the principle of grace? Where offenses abound, grace much more abounds. For where significant breaches lie, there arise a glorious opportunity for abundant reconciliation! Jesus instructed that we should forgive 70 times seven; that totals 490 times! Was this number given to provide a limit of the offenses we should endure? No! It

21

illustrates how God expects us to stop counting and take the limits off! The more offenses we suffer, the more opportunities we will have to extend mercy, and the more chances to receive God's grace in our own lives. Grace and mercy are catalysts for healing, repair, and thus reconciliation.

Pearls From Sallie's Story:

o **Be willing to initiate the conversation.**

o **Be humble—offer an apology.**

o **Ask for God's help to forgive.**

o **Face your fears and the opposition.**

o **Be longsuffering—progress, one step at a time.**

o **Remember that God's love is unconditional— pass it on!**

o **Be willing to cancel the debt; forgive!**

Reconciled to a Loving Daughter
Donna's Story

The enemy is always walking "about like a roaring lion, seeking whom he may devour" (1Peter 5:8). His aim is to make use of any opportunity or circumstance to steal, kill, and destroy. My story is of healing and restoration after many years of discord between my only daughter and me.

Divorce. It's one of the most horrific things a family can go through. Our family faced divorce when my daughter was only 12; so much heartache, suffering, and pain. The changes we endured were devastating. The children witnessed what they were too young to understand: parents splitting up, the uncertainty of the family structure, loss of feeling safe—division. My entire family was living a nightmare. The enemy had come in wreaking havoc in every area of our lives. My husband, the minister, the one who promised to love, honor, and cherish "until death, do us part," had found someone else. The marriage was over. Just as the Bible says, the devil came to steal, kill, and destroy. That's what the demise of my marriage felt like. It was stolen, killed, and destroyed before my eyes.

My husband was gone. We broke our vow. And everything in our family plummeted on a downward spiral, including my faith. The children were failing in school. The entire house suffered uncertainty, pain, and fear, challenging the relationships we worked so hard to build. How would we go on from here? Daddy's little girl lost proximity with daddy. No longer was he within arm's reach. No one could have prepared me for what came next: insolence, disobedience, rebellion. The shift was massive. This event changed the children I thought I knew so well. And for the first time, I felt the domino effect of a broken marriage—broken relationships, broken trust, and a broken home. In times past, mother and father had gotten together to fix it. But the power of our oneness existed no more. "We" became "him" and "me." What was once joined had been "put asunder." The marriage was broken and we didn't try to fix it. The children knew it. And they used our discord as an opportunity to do and get what they wanted—uncontested. They knew we would not come together and discuss things before deciding on their desires and requests. So they learned to play us against each other. Where Dad would say no, they just went to mom to hear "yes." I was so broken that I just didn't have the strength to look into the eyes of betrayal and negotiate peaceful parental decisions. Friendship—there was none. Trust—there was none. Respect—I no longer had it. Our daughter, at such a young age, stood in the middle watching the chaos. Even worse, in an innocent 12-year-old-sort of way, she was establishing a friendship with the other woman. I didn't blame her. She was a child. But after everything I had endured, I just couldn't watch it or navigate my way around it even for the sake of parental negotiations. I shifted into avoidance mode and sent my daughter to live with the decision-maker, her father.

I don't think I will ever know the total effect divorce had on my children. My daughter told me years later that she felt like I was punishing her, that the break-up was all her fault. My son never talked about it. I eventually discovered that the enemy manipulated my daughter's thinking during our separation. She had grown up believing the reason I sent her to her father's house, was because I didn't love her. I assumed that my daughter knew how much I loved her. It was a terrible mistake on my part. I didn't realize how my absence affected her. She required constant reinforcement and reassurance. I just didn't know how quickly children could lose their sense of security by watching their parent's love for each other vanish. Being an adult, I knew my love would never change. But she was a child. In her mind, the security she felt from her parents changed. And that changed everything. The divorce made her feel she was unloved. It's so sad. I never meant this to happen.

Reflection

In their book, <u>The Family: A Christian Perspective on the Contemporary Home</u>, Authors and Jack and Judith Balswick cite divorce as being higher in the United States than any other country. Unfortunately, these modern times also document the highest occurrences of divorce in human history (Balswick, 1999, p. 308). And of late, the Christian community is experiencing divorce in record numbers. Christian music artists, bishops, pastors, counselors—divorce is everywhere. How is this affecting the children long term? If you just do an internet search you'll find countless articles by experts that indicate that the jury is still out. However, talking with children, teens, and young adults who lived through their parent's divorce reveals impending feelings of insecurity, anger, rejection, and self-blame in each developmental stage. Some have great relationships with both parents. However, others became estranged from the non-custodial parent following the divorce, and that left devastating effects. In an online article on marriage and divorce by the American Psychological Association (APA), it states: "growing up in a happy home protects children from mental, physical, educational and social problems" (http://www.apa.org/topics/divorce/index.aspx), retrieved August 20, 2013. The understanding here is that growing up in less fortunate circumstances can expose children to mental, physical, educational, and social problems.

But I would like to present even another perspective: how much would children learn about commitment if they saw their parents strive to work out their differences no matter what? What would they learn about the power of forgiveness if they saw their parents work through offenses and betrayal, or broken vows? What understanding would they adopt about marriage as an institution?

It is undeniable that there are serial offenders who, make staying together impossible—having one affair after another. In these dangerous times, a life hangs in the balance of incurable disease, putting others at risk with one hasty act. Some brush it off, stating: "We just fell out of love," or "We have irreconcilable differences—we just don't get along."

What would children learn about love if they saw two mature adults work around their differences to secure the family—if they saw restraint and heard reason during troubles?

The bottom line is that decisions, actions, and lifestyles affect entire households. Each person in a family is accountable to the other. One decision made by a parent or a child can affect and reshape the identity of the entire family.

Component of Reconciliation: Communication

What is communication? By definition, it is to convey a feeling or thought, the exchange of information to understand another. We live in an era where communication is at its apex. This is evidenced through the emergence of social media. Because communication is essential to every aspect of life, you would think more people would invest in doing it more effectively. Yet poor communication continues to cause a lot of the conflict all around us. Ordinary people take their disagreements to TV judges for adjudication. Divorce is at an all-time high. And children settle for long term estrangement from their parents rather than ironing out their differences. It just makes little sense that in this day—when access to communication venues is at an all-time high—with chatting, tweeting, texting, "Instagramming," emailing, and Skyping—there is so little actual conversation, understanding, and passion for conciliation. Disagreements often remain unsettled. Some resort to arguments, violence, and guns. People like the idea of being social, but not so much when it involves meaningful conversation to avoid or resolve conflict.

For years there were uncontrollable gaps that separated people from each other. It took days just to travel a few miles or to deliver messages to family and friends in other states or countries. But now, these gaps are bridged by planes, cars, telephones, and more. Money and technology have answered every need. I talk with friends in Texas in the morning and relatives in Hawaii at night. Soldiers email their wives from Iraq. And with Apple's iPhone, you can have a face-to-face conversation from almost anywhere in the world.

COMMUNICATION SABBOTAGE:

There are, however, impairments to our effective communicating with the ones we love, work, and interact with daily. I don't think it's possible to publish an all-inclusive list, but here are just a few of the vices that sabotage the success and fruitfulness of verbal interactions:

Masks

The only way that two people can come together and achieve fruitful dialogue is that both parties take off their masks and get real with each other. Let's face it; impressions can drive our relationships. We care if people perceive us as weak or fragile. "Don't let them see you cry." The adage, "Sticks and stones may break my bones, but words will never hurt me," is not valid. Words hurt sometimes to the very core of the soul. But rather than saying, "What you said hurt me," many people leave hurtful dialogue unaddressed, allowing it to fester until it builds into something too great to ignore. Anger, resentment, bitterness— emotional maladies that have the potential to defile the heart. *Looking diligently lest any man fail of the grace of God; lest any root of bitterness springing up trouble you, and thereby many be defiled. (Hebrews 12:15)*

What is the "root of bitterness?" By definition, bitterness comprises anger, disappointment, and resentment. It becomes embedded so deep that it's hidden until it grows and breaks through the surface. Just as tree roots grow underground, bursting forth to reveal its bark, stems, and leaves, so bitterness becomes a mighty force that can shatter the heart. Tree roots can be so strong that they break through concrete to give freedom to budding arms. No one wants his heart to break by the force of bitterness and its many branches of strongholds.

Bitterness can be avoided by dealing with disappointment and anger as quickly and completely as possible. False apologies and guarded conversations will not facilitate resolution. The Apostle Paul used the word "dissimulation," which means inauthentic—fake. He instructed the Romans to live without counterfeit love.

Let love be without dissimulation. Abhor that which is evil; cleave to that which is good. Be kindly affectioned one to another with brotherly love; in honour preferring one another. (Romans 12:9-10)

Masks become the device of choice to a) avoid dealing with conflict and dreaded truths between people, b) maintain relationships with meaningful people regardless of persisting personal issues. We could ask the question, "Can two walk together in dissimulation?" Here's a new, unfamiliar word that describes the coexistence of love and hate in a relationship—"frenemy!" A frenemy exhibits two sides of character, one that is likable, and the other that is obnoxious. His role seems consistent until he finds cause for envy or jealousy—for which cause the "frenemy" both admires and resents his friend. These feelings can lead these sometimes haters to sabotage the individual. On the surface, the two friends have a harmonious relationship. However, beneath the surface, there is profound dissimulation and undermining in the shadows.

The story of David and Saul in 1 Samuel 17-18 illustrates this duplicitous state between friends. As a youth, David had the faith and courage to challenge the undefeated champion of the Philistines, Goliath, the giant. Incensed by Goliath's arrogance and taunting of the Israelites, David took personal offense that anyone would dare challenge the Lord's army: "Who is this uncircumcised Philistine, that he should defy the armies of the living God?" (1

Samuel 17:26). When Saul heard these words, he sent for David, only to discover that he talked like a fearless warrior, even though he was just a spry young teen. "Thy servant will go and fight with this Philistine" (1 Samuel 17:32). Imagine Saul's face. Here was a teenager, unmoved and unafraid to face this menace to their society. There were no weapons, no armor, or intimidating muscles with which to overthrow the buxom combatant. Saul tried to convince him of his vulnerability; he was but a youth. He was no soldier, but a shepherd unequipped to go against a skilled mighty warrior with years of training and experience. But he could not discourage David. Saul's argument presented David with the opportunity to reveal his resume. David was young, but he was no weakling. Nor was he a coward. As a young shepherd he saved a sheep from being devoured by a lion:

"And David said unto Saul, thy servant kept his father's sheep, and there came a lion, and a bear, and took a lamb out of the flock: And I went out after him, and smote him, and delivered it out of his mouth: and when he arose against me, I caught him by his beard, and smote him, and slew him" (1Samuel 17:33-35). His story did not end there. David had not only slain a lion, but a bear also, and he intended to add Goliath to the mantle of collected animal heads! In David's eyes, the great Philistine champion was not even as fierce as the animals he had already defeated—with his bare hands no less! Who would not admire such valor? In conclusion, David kept his word. He defeated Goliath. His choice weapon, a slingshot! He then removed the giant's head with his own sword. From that day forward, Saul commanded David to

leave his father's house and come to the palace. As a reward, Saul set him over the men of war, a position David wore with wisdom and much favor in the kingdom.

So what changed in this relationship of great admiration, trust, and respect? There was one life changing event. David was returning home from yet another successful battle campaign. As he entered the city the women greeted their champions with music and a song: *"Saul hath slain his thousands, and David his ten thousand!" (1 Samuel 18:7).* From the moment Saul heard that song, he realized that David far succeeded his esteem, celebrity, and eminence in the kingdom. A seed of jealousy grew, *"And Saul eyed David from that day and forward" (1 Samuel 18:9).* Had David changed? No, he still served and respected his king. But Saul, even with all the admiration he once held for David, had a changed heart toward his friend. Saul became jealous. And as David played the harp by his side, just as he had many times before, Saul did the unthinkable; he threw a javelin at him! It was in that revealing moment that David recognized Saul's true feelings: it was admiration gone sour. Saul's jealousy trumped the former love and respect he once had for David. Alas, King Saul was unmasked!

You can't contrive genuine love: it is real, unconditional, and spontaneous.

Hasty Words

Wherefore, my beloved brethren, let every man be swift to hear, slow to speak, slow to wrath: For the wrath of man worketh not the righteousness of God (James 1:19-20).

Have you ever found yourself in a conversation that got away from you? Well, I have. The conversation seemed to go fine, then something happened. Someone said something offensive or just plain wrong. Then everything went south. Somehow in conversation, things can get jumbled, or lost, or even burped out before it hits the brain's filter. What then?

There is no script for our conversations, so it's imperative that we use excellent communication skills: a listening ear, quick thinking, a functional vocabulary, and restraint! If you know the person well, you have enough history and understanding to decipher the murkiest of dialogue. Even then, however, you can still experience times when you take a hit for saying the wrong thing!

One of the greatest lessons we can learn as communicators is that words have power. It's better to say little and listen much, rather than doing a whole lot of talking, particularly when the relationship is fragile. People become very vulnerable when conflict looms. One hasty remark could tip the scale. There's nothing wrong with saying, "This is a sensitive subject. I need to think about it." Or, "I'm upset about this. I need to clear my head for a while." Or the most candid response: "I'm angry! It's better if I don't talk about this now!"

Being honest and truthful during sensitive times will both spare and deliver all parties from hasty words, hurt feelings, and fractured relationships.

Honesty and restraint are loyal friends of meaningful communication.

Broken Rules

There's something very similar about hasty words and broken rules—both tend to hit below the belt! "I never should have married you!" Or "I don't know why I had children!" Let's face it; once you say it, you can never take it back! You can feel so angry that you think you see red, but that time will pass. What you don't want is to come to yourself, only to see a blazing trail of casualties you knocked off with your words. The spouse you love and adore will have a shattered heart. Your children, your little darlings, will always wonder if you are glad they were born. When you break the rules in the heat of anger, you can damage the people you love. You can apologize, but the damage must heal.

Some things should never be said period.

Pain

Watching a woman in labor is an excellent illustration of how pain can affect communication. Sitcoms depict these women as going ballistic on their husbands, proclaiming, "I hate you," one minute and "I love you" the next. Yet the birth of a child is undeniably one of the happiest times a couple will experience. Despite the physical pain, once the little bundle of joy arrives, biting words, tears, and anguish cease as the focus shifts to new life.

But there are other times when pain does not produce a happy ending. I have lost my father to heart disease, uncles to cancer, and even an endeared cousin in the tragedy on 9/11. I broke my jaw when I was in college, which resulted in having my mouth wired shut for over three months; and had two c-sections when my children were born. I've mourned, suffered a broken heart, broken bones, and had several incisions. After each physical and emotional hardship, I put a lot of effort towards becoming strong again. Pain can affect the way we act and react to life and the people in it. Pain and suffering can cause us to feel overwhelmed, irrational, and emotional. It can move us to say things and make decisions we will surely regret.

Everyone has a unique way of handling pain. I have met people with a high tolerance for physical pain, but others who shut down if they just get a headache. I've met people who experienced the betrayal of adultery and later reconciled their marriages, becoming more cohesive and successful than ever before. But others that divorced and continued to spew venom for the rest of their lives. Pain affects people, relationships, and the journeys of life. It therefore becomes a critical factor in the reconciliation process. That's why it is so important to know and understand how pain affects you. It's during those times, when life hurts, that you must be intentional to act and not react when dealing with loved ones. The pain will pass. You'll feel better. And you'll see your world and people in it through clearer lenses.

Pain can alter the truth.

Fear of Rejection

Have you ever wanted to disclose something personal about yourself but feared that if people knew the real you, they would judge or reject you? Well, you aren't alone. As a pastor's wife, my role was that of spiritual mother and mentor to the congregants. Yet I had numerous encounters of unexplained rejection. It took me a while to recognize the pattern. So many of the women were estranged from their natural mothers. There had been excessive criticism, fault-finding, ignoring, so many vices that left them broken and uninterested in being "mothered." As I listened to their stories, I began to see the pattern and I finally understood—detachment was their paradigm. This was an undeniable common thread many of them never recognized as a factor stunting their emotional journey. Instead of dealing with it they put up barriers with "mother figures," leaning to their own understanding or resorting to peers for counsel. That felt like a safe place, but in reality, it was a dangerous one. There can be no safety without wisdom: *"Wisdom is a defence…wisdom giveth life to them that have it" (Ecclesiastes 7:12).* People need significant individuals in their lives whose very presence forces them to grow and to deal with hard issues, unexpected afflictions, and character flaws—we all have them! But many forgo such relationships fearing the consequences of disclosure and nakedness.

It takes courage to let people into the secret place of private disclosure. Let's face it, you may take a hit for being so candid about yourself. Everyone can't handle the truth (that famous line from the movie "A Few Good Men" was revelatory). But there will be some who will amaze you by listening and giving you a shoulder to cry on—loving you unconditionally. All you need is one person! When you find them, that's when you will discover how stagnating fear pales compared to the progress you will experience when you take a risk.

Fear stagnates, while courage is a conduit to progress.

Obstinance

What is obstinance? If you look it up you'll discover that it's not often used. It describes a person who is self-willed, stubborn, and pig-headed, one who adheres to their own ideas or desires. It is not good to be obstinate for these characteristics also reveal an air of being unmovable, unaffected, and even unteachable.

This attitude is one of the greatest saboteurs of communication. The prevailing mindset of an obstinate person is: "Nothing you say can or will move me!" They determine to maintain their view, their stance, and their resolve. No matter what you say or how long you talk, they will remain unaffected by the information you disclose. They cannot glean wisdom or meaningful revelations. They will not budge even if you bear your heart, explain why you acted as you did, or reveal the history that led to your actions or decisions. It's tough to reason or reconcile with an obstinate person because their view is the only view.

BIBLE VERSES ABOUT OBSTINANCE:

1Peter 5:5
"Likewise, ye younger, submit yourselves unto the elder. Yea, all of you be subject one to another, and be clothed with humility: for God resisteth the proud, and giveth grace to the humble."

Proverbs 13:18
Poverty and shame shall be to him that refuseth instruction: but he that regardeth reproof shall be honoured.

Proverbs 12:1
Whoso loveth instruction loveth knowledge: but he that hateth reproof is brutish.

2 Timothy 3:1-4
This know also, that in the last days perilous times shall come. For men shall be lovers of their own selves, covetous, boasters, proud, blasphemers, disobedient to parents, unthankful, unholy, Without natural affection, trucebreakers, false accusers, incontinent, fierce, despisers of those that are

good, Traitors, heady, highminded, lovers of pleasures more than lovers of God;
These verses bring to light some very pointed characteristics about the obstinate person:

1. There is a stark contrast between humility and pride; God resists the proud (I Peter 5:5).

2. Refusing instruction brings poverty and shame and dishonor (Proverbs 13:18).

3. Loving instruction manifests love for knowledge. Hating it is akin to choosing ignorance. Hating correction, criticism, rebuke (reproof), identifies one as being loutish or lacking refinement and intelligence (Proverbs 12:1).

4. Choosing to love oneself, pride and highmindedness are some of the characteristics of people in the last days. We are witnessing this now! Just a few insights on the word "highminded:" it includes being saucy, sassy, and disrespectful.

These verses reveal how talking to an obstinate person can be very difficult, sabotaging good intentions. Such a one is not interested in empathizing with the views of another. They don't feel they can learn anything because they know it all. The obstinate has no problem saying whatever comes to mind, even if their words are biting and hurtful.

When you recognize evidence of obstinance, the most you can do is pray for grace in the reconciliation encounter; say what you need to say and be at peace. Release it. Forgive. And walk away. No expectations. No offense.

The obstinate will not change, but if you overlook their attitude, you will!

Denial

The ostrich is one of the most common symbols of denial. This animal's stance of, putting his head in a hole, illustrates people who refuse to face painful realities. In defense of this animal, however, the holes they dig have much more purpose than escaping reality. Their holes actually provide a safe place for their young. Likewise, people bury their heads in figurative holes to feel safe, but the real goal is avoidance. Caller ID is one example. It affords us the power to choose: do I want to talk to you? If the answer is YES—I will answer. If the answer is NO—I won't!

Denial goes even deeper than avoidance. Denial says, "My phone is not ringing!" People who experience denial refuse to face the fact that a situation or problem exists. Therefore, they don't recognize or accept the need to reconcile. I have seen this work in two distinct ways:

Denial Example One
The person has convinced himself that the relationship is just fine, despite the warning signs—they refuse to face it.

Denial Example Two

The person says that things are fine because they don't want to deal with any altercation or conflict—so they refuse to openly acknowledge that a problem exists.

Whichever the case, denial can hinder effective communication that could lead to truth and pure harmony in a relationship.

Excellent relationships can only grow when individuals determine to face problems head-on and solve them.

> ***Denial leaves issues unresolved and problems unanswered.***

Anger

Reality shows today showcase unscripted shouting matches, expletive dialogue and physical aggression between angry people. Never before have we witnessed such private encounters on nationwide television. Even the youth have video games that make sport of violent and destructive contests that engage their emotions, instincts, and reflexes more than their intellect. They can pick up a video game and experience gang violence, anarchy, murder, and mayhem from the safety of their bedrooms. Road rage is prevailing among parents and bullying among students. People are acting out in anger. And because of it, we are experiencing increased occurrences of beatings, shootings, and other cruel acts of violence among adults and children who are becoming desensitized to the evils of wrath. I even hear Christians quoting the Scripture, *"be angry, and sin not: let not the sun go down upon your wrath"(Ephesians 4:26),* as excuses for relinquishing their temperament to bursts of anger.

I attended a funeral for an individual who was shot at close range after an altercation during a heated game. He never lived to see his thirties. I have seen youth suffer great depression after being bullied in school. And road rage—I could write an entire chapter about that! One specific incident that comes to mind was an event that happened to my daughter and me one chilly winter night. We were driving down a major road when my headlights malfunctioned. The only thing I could think to do was try my bright lights. What a relief to discover that I still had bright lights. I was relieved, but the driver in front of me became outraged. He slowed down and got over into the lane next to me. What ensued after that was frightening. He drove close beside me, jerked over in front of me, then jammed on his brakes so I would have no choice but to jam on my brakes or slam into his bumper. I almost lost control of the car! When I changed lanes, he changed lanes behind me. He followed me for miles! I sped up, trying to lose him. But he stayed with me. It felt like a scene from an action movie. Except I was no stunt driver and his rage definitely was not scripted. Finally, I got to a significant fork in the road. God gave me a plan: stay in the far right lane—he would prepare himself to follow me into town. The left lane was the entrance to the freeway. I continued driving in the right lane. At the last minute, just where the road divided, I jerked over into the left lane, taking the freeway. It was an unexpected maneuver that left my assailant behind on the right road into town. We got away. God made a way of escape! My daughter was completely terrified. As our hearts pounded, I thanked God for delivering us. It was so senseless. One moment of anger could have prevented us from getting home that night. But God!

What does the Bible say about anger? Look at the second clause of Ephesians 4:26: *"Sin not: let not the sun go down upon your wrath."* Many quote this verse but, few regard the instruction, *"Sin not,"* or the rest of the verse, *"let not the sun go down upon your wrath."*

What this verse is telling us is this; anger is an emotion we will sometimes experience. Allowing that anger to rule or become the cause for sinful actions that wrong others, now that's a problem. Neither should we allow anger to persist from one day into the next. Tomorrow is not promised to us.

Anger is a natural emotion. But the Word of God does indeed provide helpful insights to help us to deal with this emotion and the people who provoke it. Here are just a few scriptures on anger; please note the consistencies in both the Old and New Testaments!

BIBLE VERSES ABOUT ANGER:

Psalms 37:8	Refrain from anger
Proverbs 14:29 & 15:18 & James 1:19-20	Be slow to anger
Proverbs 29:22 & 30:33	The angry stir up strife
Proverbs 14:16-17 & Ecclesiastes 7:9	Fools rage
Proverbs 19:11	Put off (defer) anger
Matthew 5:21-24	Jesus' teaching on anger: anger without cause puts you in danger of judgment.
Galatians 5:19-25	Paul's teaching on anger: wrath is of the flesh as opposed to the fruit of the spirit.
Colossians 3:8-13	Paul's teaching on anger: put off anger and wrath.

Just looking at these scriptures, it is easy to see how anger can sabotage communication. Anger can affect the very words chosen to express your position in a relationship. Anger can cause your words to "stir up strife," as opposed to appeasing it. Friction, discord, and fighting will not create an atmosphere conducive to healing a broken relationship. It's not good to attempt a reconciliation encounter if you are too angry to control your temperament or words.

Angry communication can further fracture a relationship.

Donna's Story Continued: Where is my Daughter?

After the divorce, something became broken between my daughter and me. We lost that closeness and became more like strangers. Though we shared moments, none of these included heartfelt talks. Like other mothers and daughters, we didn't talk about hopes and dreams or feelings and fears. The relationship felt very disconnected and superficial.

It wasn't until many years later that my daughter revealed some of her deepest feelings with me; she had grown up feeling indifferent about her welfare. She made decisions lightly and destructively. She concealed how little she valued herself. And though she hid her inner-most thoughts, what was visible was a cold and uncaring young lady. I guess I always thought the divorce was behind her demeanor; even after our family had parted ways, and I became friends with my ex-husband, my daughter never came around. Our relationship never quite felt restored. We were just "okay."

I always wanted more but never had the nerve to pursue it. I lost a lot of time desiring it and doing nothing about it. That is until my daughter turned 19. Finally, for some reason, I got up the nerve to ask for "the talk." And I didn't beat around the bush either. I let her know up-front that I wanted to have an open conversation that would heal us beyond just being "okay." I said, "If I can just say some things out loud, to reveal my true feelings the devil won't own it anymore." She agreed to meet. This talk was our first discussion about the past, about the divorce, and what it had done to us. She had lived with her father for years without having an open intentional dialogue with me. Finally, she shared the feelings she kept secret for so many years, her darkest feelings. She thought I didn't love her because I sent her to live with her father. It was hard to hear. We talked long and hard that day, ambivalent to our restaurant surroundings. We laid all our feelings out. All that time, one decision had severed our closeness. All I could do was assure my daughter how much I loved her—truly loved her all along. And offer my heartfelt apology for the misunderstanding. She was so glad that we talked. We both were. We prayed together. Right there. And that's when the healing began.

Sometime after, I don't recall how long, my pastor preached a sermon entitled, "The Power of Forgiveness." From the moment I heard that message, I felt pressed to ask my daughter's forgiveness. Not just to say, "I'm sorry," as I had done previously, but to humbly seek her forgiveness for my part in her pain and suffering growing up. The Lord showed me that it didn't matter how it happened or what my motives were. She was suffering and it was because of a decision I had made. For the first time, I felt the far-reaching consequences my actions imposed upon my daughter. The divorce had caused me pain, but being an adult, I mustered up the fortitude to deal with it. My daughter, however, continued to suffer throughout her developing years—from childhood into womanhood.

God's Spirit wouldn't let me rest. And I was in a hurry to obey. Sunday's sermon became Monday's pursuit of resolution. I called my daughter and told her that I needed to talk to her again. "Are you serious?" My daughter laughed at my request. I laughed too, as I explained that I had left out some critical details when we talked before. She promised to come that very day. I cried, thanking God for his mercy and for showing me what I need to do.

Together At Last

It was Monday afternoon. She knocked. As I opened the door, we both started laughing simultaneously. "Ma, I don't believe this!" She was light-hearted and welcoming. I was glad. "What I have to say is really important." I needed her to understand how serious I was about our meeting. We sat down at the kitchen table

47

to share tea and sandwiches. We set the stage with small talk. The atmosphere felt right and ready. I reached over and took her hand and began to tell her again how sorry I was for all her pain and suffering as a little girl; she needed her mother, and I wasn't there as I should have been. I asked if she could forgive me for making her feel unloved and unwanted. She tried to laugh through her tears. I guess to lighten the moment. "I forgive you, Ma."

It was a very important step on our journey toward reconciliation. It took us some time after that day. And somewhere along the way, my daughter gave birth to a son, whom I love dearly. Today I can honestly say that our mother-daughter bond has finally been restored. I give credit to the Lord, but I believe, also to my grandson, whom God added as another bridge to the gap in our relationship. Now, my daughter doesn't hesitate to call me for advice: "Ma, what should I do— what do you think...?" I'm thankful that she trusts me enough to not only ask, but to follow my advice in raising her son. This trust has also grown over the years to include seeking my counsel regarding her personal matters as well. My response to her is always driven by my desire to please God, following His word—not my own personal view. She seems to appreciate that.

I know the Lord reconciled me to my daughter through the power of forgiveness, which I learned needed to be sought without excuses. I am humbled and grateful for the restoration and rekindled relationship I desired for so long. In fact, God has done even more that I expected; true to His word, He has not just restored the relationship, but also the years that were stolen.

It's not easy to receive the Lord's correction. But I now realize the importance of accepting responsibility for wrong actions and following the Lord's instructions to make it right. I give glory to God for empowering me to submit to humble myself before my daughter. And now I am reaping the benefits every day in the name of Jesus Christ. Amen

Reconciliation requires humility.

Pearls From Donna's Story:

o Always tell your children how much you love them—especially when your family is facing troubles.

o Face your fears.

o Work hard to keep the lines of communication open.

o Be honest about your failures, seek forgiveness.

o Talk from the heart.

o Be humble.

o Respect the feelings of others—your view is not the only view!

o Receive the Lord's correction and instruction.

o Stop making excuses for leaving essential relationships broken.

"The Boiling Point" by Crystal McGriff

How long does it take for water to boil?
Every ill word spoken, every verbal attack, was increasing
the fire in the eye....
Low, to medium, to high
Less and less words spoken, until the day you just simply
walk on by.
The boiling begins...

Emotions of hurt, anger, and retaliation spins
It grows until it surfaces, becoming manifest for all to see
and hear.
Relationship molding

Words and actions triggered reactions,
Shots fired by the tongue.
Two people, one right, it seems the battle just begun.
Two wrongs, no right
No right but one.
Who will be bold enough to humble themselves?

Forgiveness can feel like blows to the chest.
But, in reality it's blows to the flesh.
To forgive is to be forgiven.
If you're living in anger, hate, and unforgiveness...
Then you're not living.
Let the flesh die.

Set aside those things that had you so angry and love.

Let God heal the wounds that led to the pain.

Remove the water.

Reduce the heat.

Settle. Resolve. Reunite. Patch Up.

Whatever synonym speaks to that part of you that wants to reconcile.

Whatever word that encourages you to see past the outside.

In this world, life is timed. Tomorrow is conditional. Today is opportunity. Yesterday is lost.

What will you do with the opportunity, not to live with tomorrow's regrets?

Take advantage of your yesterday being today.

Forgive. Love. Reconcile.

The Year My Sister Became My Friend
Charlotte's Story

"Sometimes, things have to get turned upside down before they become right side up!" It sounds like an oxymoron, but in my life, this saying has proven to be true. I remember the exact date, June 29, 2001. Every predictable thing in my life gave way to chaos. I attended a special service at our church, featuring a guest pastor and his congregation. I'll never forget what he preached: "The Set Time and The Appointed Time of God." His message was a foretelling of events to come. He boldly declared, "God is going to allow your lives to be turned upside down for a season, but by the time He turns things right side up again, every prayer and written request will be answered!" That preacher didn't know it, but I had a lot of requests written on my prayer cards. It was a great time of rejoicing for me. All of my petitions were about to be fulfilled! All I could think about was my written request for my family to be saved and my one heart's desire--that I would have the true "sister-friend" relationship of my dreams. I longed for my sister to be in my life again.

I am the oldest of four siblings. We are equally gendered, two boys and two girls. So I have two brothers, but only one sister; she's my junior by six years. Growing up, she was scrawny. Yet bold, rambunctious, and always surrounded by playful boys, especially with our middle brother. We called the two of them, "The middle kids."

53

Being the oldest and less prone to mischief, Mom left me in charge when she was away. I hated getting into trouble, so I tried to do everything right to make life easier for Mom. I worked hard at being and giving my best. A quality that identified me as "goody-two-shoes." While my siblings and peers thought I was a real square, adults seemed to applaud me as a good example. That was good and bad. Good because Mom recognized my efforts to live right. But it was bad because she often lauded my successes to my siblings, "Why can't you be more like your sister Charlotte?" I started noticing a real change in my sister's attitude toward me. I honestly believe it was a direct result of her feeling measured by me.

Reflection

Have you ever felt like you were wearing a "coat of many colors?" Well, there was one young man who did—Joseph. Genesis chapters 29-50 tells his story. It started with his father, Jacob, meeting a beautiful woman, his cousin Rachel. Jacob desired to marry her. But her older sister, Leah, was not yet married.

Nevertheless, Laban agreed to accept Jacob's offer to earn Rachel's hand by working for him for seven years. The morning after the blissful wedding night, Jacob arose to discover that his bride was not the fair Rachel, but the elder daughter, tender-eyed Leah. His conniving uncle, Laban, had deceived him by concealing Leah's identity and giving her hand in marriage instead of Rachel's.

"And it came to pass, that in the morning, behold, it was Leah: and he said to Laban, What is this thou hast done unto me? did not I serve with thee for Rachel? wherefore then hast thou beguiled me? And Laban said, It must not be so done in our country, to give the younger before the firstborn. Fulfil her week, and we will give thee this also for the service which thou shalt serve with me yet seven other years" (Genesis 29:25-27).

So Jacob endured the week with Leah, eager to marry Rachel in seven days, with a deal to stay and work another seven years in return for Rachel's hand. It was a painful time for Leah, witnessing the true love Jacob had for her sister. God, graciously seeing her pain determined to bless her: *"And when the Lord saw that Leah was hated, he opened her womb: but Rachel was barren" (Genesis 29:31).* Time after time, Leah conceived, believing that with the birth of each son, Jacob would love her. And four sons later, she faced the painful truth; Rachel remained the favored wife—even without producing one single child. Jacob loved her unconditionally.

This scenario lent to conditions ripe for jealousy between the two sisters. Genesis 30:1 states, "Rachel envied her sister." She wanted a child. But she had a problem—she had not been able to conceive. She blamed her husband: *"Give me children, or else I die" (Genesis 30:1).* He sharply put her in check: *"Am I in God's stead, who hath withheld from thee the fruit of the womb?"(Genesis 30:2).* Rachel went from envying her sister to blaming her husband.

With that response, Rachel determined to rectify her plight by giving her husband her handmaid, who bore Jacob two sons. The contest between the sisters continued; Leah, now barren after four sons, also sent her handmaid into Jacob, who also birthed two sons, bringing the count to eight sons! They were out of control, playing Jacob like a ping-pong-ball in a sports match. This rivalry continued between the sisters until Leah had a total of six sons. The birth of her daughter, Dinah, became the cycle breaker in this continuing saga.

"And God remembered Rachel, and God hearkened to her, and opened her womb. And she conceived, and bare a son; and said, God hath taken away my reproach: And she called his name Joseph; and said, The Lord shall add to me another son" *(Genesis 30:22-24).*

Jacob's story is an excellent example of life turned "upside down." He saw a pretty girl and imagined a blissful life with her. But the reality exceeded his imagination. He found himself lingering with Laban for 14 years, marrying two sisters, and birthing ten children by four women! Laban tricked him, entrapping him in a web of envy, that catapulted him into the clutches of a real-life "sex-opera!" But through it all, Jacob was thrilled when Rachel bore her firstborn son, Joseph. Surely with his arrival, life would begin to turn right side up again. Wrong. Where Leah and Rachel plagued their house with envy and competition, Jacob became the catalyst of even more discord in his family:

"Now Israel (Jacob) loved Joseph more than all his children, because he was the son of his old age: and he made him a coat of many colours. And when his brethren saw that their father loved him more than all his brethren, they hated him, and could not speak peaceably unto him" (Genesis 37:3-4).

Finally, Jacob had a son, Joseph, an heir from his most beloved Rachel. And all the other children knew he was the favored child. To top it off, he wore the token of Jacob's preference for all to see—"a coat of many colors!" It's quite a story. His brothers, gripped by jealousy, conspired to be rid of Joseph; they stripped him of his colorful coat, dipped it in goat's blood, and threw him in a pit. But rather than leaving him for death to take, they instead bargained with the slave-trading Ishmaelites to own him for 20 pieces of silver (Genesis 37:18-28). The brothers delivered the bloody shredded coat to their father, leaving him to think the worst:

"And they sent the coat of many colours, and they brought it to their father; and said, This have we found: know now whether it be thy son's coat or no. And he knew it, and said, It is my son's coat; an evil beast hath devoured him; Joseph is without doubt rent in pieces" (Genesis 37:32-33).

So as Leah hated her sister Rachel for being Jacob's favorite wife, so did Leah's sons hate Joseph for being their father's most beloved son. And the symbol of partiality was used to issue the final blow. The coat of many colors—alas—the shredded coat, became the visible emblem of favoritism destroyed.

Do you wear a coat of many colors in your family?

Charlotte's Story Continued

As a child, people called me "Goody-two-shoes." In high school, I was called "Miss Perfectionist." Then in college, I was nick-named, "Ms. Right-is-Right." By the year 2001, the Lord had truly saved and sanctified me; I was baptized in the name of the Lord Jesus Christ and filled with the gift of the Holy Ghost. His favor was upon me; He opened doors. I traveled to France as a French exchange student. I was on the honor roll, an athlete, cheerleader captain, and on the "Who's Who of High School Students" list. I was accepted to the Naval Academy at Annapolis and many universities and was a scholarship recipient. I proceeded into college, declaring a double major in Electrical Engineering and Mathematics and graduated from the University of Connecticut on the Dean's List. From there, I went on to become an engineer and ultimately, vested, and promoted through the ranks, succeeding to supervisor and a traveling corporate manager. I had just purchased a new car and was contemplating buying a house for $40,000.00 cash. I paid a substantial five-figure amount in tithes to my home church. Some people would say I had it "going on." God gave me favor. But that did not exempt me from trouble.

I had left that church service feeling so confirmed in the Word. I just knew that God would answer my prayers. Nothing could have prepared me for what happened next. On Monday, July 2, 2001, without warning, I went to work and received a pink slip. Just like that, my job was gone. I was out of work for 18 months. It was a time of humbling. I had known the favor of God, but during the layoff, I found just how little I knew the God that I served. I knew that He saved me, justified me, and gave me knowledge and understanding of His word. I even realized that all of my abilities and favor came from Him. But something very essential was missing. I still needed to learn how to be like Christ, approachable, touchable, both human and godly simultaneously. While striving for perfection in the eyes of man, and increasing in worldly and spiritual knowledge, I had missed the main thing. That broke me.

For the first time in my life, I was the one who needed help. And that fact seemed to beckon my sister to come. It was almost as if she needed to be needed if that makes sense. She started writing me letters and calling from time to time. I was happy that she cared enough to talk to me. Though it probably made it easier for her to reach out, remembering that I had surprised her with a car when she graduated! But that wasn't it at all; for the first time, I shared my struggles with her. And seeing how I engaged in the fight gave her hope. It was the first time she saw me as human, fallible, and imperfect, yet still a believer. That gave her something to relate to. And she began to understand that being saved was not about effortless perfection after all.

Component of Reconciliation: Transparency

"Now that we are both adults, I want to get to know you better." When I read that letter from my sister, the one I longed to be close to, I saw a glimmer of hope. I was even more determined to proceed with my prayers, seeking wisdom and love. Virtues I learned to pursue during my unemployment storm.

Being estranged, I had conceded to sending gifts and cards. But my sister's letters drew me into replacing my mailers with live visits. We talked. And I found that for the first time, I wanted to hear her opinions and advice. I loved her right where she was, thanking God for every opportunity to interact with her. God gave me wise words that seemed to encourage her, and to draw her closer to Him. Before long, I was able to ask her to forgive me, and I forgave her. We both wanted a new beginning.

Reconciliation requires vulnerability.

I went to see my sister again for Christmas. And having a more open relationship allowed her to confide her intention to move in with her new fiancé. They had been dating for six months. Talking to them really increased my concern for them both. Neither went to church. My soon to be brother in law explained that he didn't go because there were so many hypocrites in his family growing up. As delicately and truthfully as I could, I encouraged him to be part of the solution; they should get married before moving in together. They needed a church where they could learn how to live right, pleasing the Lord. Asking it as a favor, I invited them to attend a church service while I was visiting—we would pick the church together. A cousin recommended a new church we could all try together. They accepted the invitation and came with me.

I was determined to dawn an innocuous persona, so my sister and her fiancé would feel comfortable. But God had another idea. The praises were so high that I found myself on the floor near the altar for most of the service. I didn't want them to label me a "holy-roller," or to think I was putting on antics. I wanted them to know that I was having an authentic experience with God. So I prayed. Right there, from the floor: "Lord, show them that your spirit is real, meet them before they leave this service." I cast all my care on Him and continued to bless Him.

Reflection

Intercessory prayer is a powerful tool. It draws the heart into the Lord's presence on behalf of someone else. 1 Timothy 2:1 reads: *"I exhort therefore, that, first of all, supplications, prayers, intercessions, and giving of thanks, be made for all men."*

There will be times during the process of reconciliation when words just won't be enough. You can talk to people. They can read books and even get counseling. But until there is an eye-opening revelation, an "aha!" moment, they won't move forward. There will always be questions: "What if I say the wrong thing?" or "What if I am the only one who wants to reconcile?" The most significant revelation on the road to reconciliation is discovering that you must become empowered to give unconditional love. And that empowerment happens in the heart. Intercessory prayer can touch the human heart where words may not. That common saying, "She had a sudden change of heart," can become a reality when you pray for God to move upon the heart.

We live in an age where people are engaging in "self-help." But let's face it; if we could help ourselves, we wouldn't require so much help to begin with. We create many of our own problems from the choices we make, the relationships we forge, and the wrong that we do. Prayer is the most effective tool humans have on earth! Through prayer, we communicate with the true and living God! We can release our hurts and our fears to one who has the wisdom and power to help in time of trouble. Through prayer, we can petition for help in stressful and dangerous situations and get immediate and lasting results.

I remember when I was a youthful woman, pregnant with my first child. It was a hot steamy summer day. I was returning from my routine visit with the doctor. Everything was fine, and I received an excellent report. Taking my usual route on I-75, I was driving in the fast lane when something went wrong with my car. I made it to the right shoulder just before the car stopped. It was 98 degrees, and there I was, stuck on the side of the road. Back then, we didn't have cell phones, so my first thought was that either some stranger would stop, or I would be stranded in a hot car, pregnant, and scared. I prayed: "Lord, send someone I know to help me!" It was a brief prayer, but very specific. Within minutes, a sister from my church pulled up behind me! Five minutes! My car was still cold from the air conditioner that ceased minutes earlier! The sister said she was on the service drive above, looked down, and recognized my car on the shoulder below. She took me for help and I was back on my way in what felt like 30 minutes! As it turned out, my gas gage malfunctioned and my tank was actually empty. All I needed was gas. My faith grew leaps that day. I learned how personally God extends His love to us. He is waiting to meet our needs, and yes, to restore our relationships. He often uses people to do it! We just need to ask.

Charlotte's Story Continued

God Answered My Prayer!

Still, on the floor overwhelmed by the Spirit, God was moving in me. But he was also dealing with my sister and her future husband. They later told me how the pastor beckoned for them to come to the pulpit and prophesied to them about their future children. He spoke to my future brother-in-law about his secrets — giving him wisdom and direction on how to handle them. God blew their minds! They came out believing.

They have been going to church since. From that day forward, they have both treated me like a favorite sister, friend, and confidant.

Reconciliation requires prayers and intercession.

Revelations

I never knew it, but I had been hindering my relationship with my sister. Not so much with my words, but with my actions. God really dealt with me while I was unemployed. During that testing period, I had an eye-opening revelation; without that woeful test, I would never have become transparent and humble before God and other people. It was liberating. No longer did I feel that I had to project a "Perfect Christian" image. I don't know when it happened, but I had become one of those mask-wearing believers with a big "S" on my chest—"Super saint"—that was me! I could understand why so many sinners thought many believers to be hypocrites.

People need encounters with someone who can relate to their hardships, feel their pain, and have made it through the press of suffering. They need to not only see the triumph, but the journey traveled to get there. For the first time, I understood the significance of the phrase, "Suffering Saviour".

"For we have not an high priest which cannot be touched with the feeling of our infirmities; but was in all points tempted like as we are, yet without sin" (Hebrews 4:15).

64

Jesus openly endured the same pain we experience: hunger, heartache, grief, weariness, anger, betrayal, and even poverty—not having a home to call His own. Yet He remained ever-loving, faithful, and true to His cause and to His God. Facing temptation, He remained pure. Being all-powerful, He remained humble. He healed the sick, cleansed the lepers, and raised the dead. Yet that same Jesus found time to attend a wedding, weep for the dead, and embrace little children. The multitudes loved Him. Children sought after Him. Even sinners let down their walls to talk to Him. And when soldiers scourged, and pierced Him, everyone saw His wounds. After all He had done to uplift, free, and deliver souls afflicted with sickness and spirits it was evident; He was divine. It was His compassion and suffering, however, that revealed that He was also oh, so human.

Who had I become? Self-righteous, refusing to let people see my scars or hear the negative side of my testimony though I had no problem sharing my victories. I had been prideful, self-sufficient, and a provider of needs, but refusing the same when offered to me. Rescuing others felt good to me. Yet I never realized how uncomfortable I made others feel, judging them whenever they slipped into sin. And I had an unforgiving heart, holding onto whatever offenses (real or imagined) committed against me. I had made my sister a hostage to her transgressions. My eyes became opened, and I did not like what God forced me to see.

Little did I realize that these painful revelations were opening my eyes to maturity, self-examination, and forgiveness. It was time to stop hiding my mistakes, confess my flaws, repent of my sin, and grant the people in my life the room to grow.

I never accused my sister to her face, but I harbored it in my heart. And that became my offense toward her. So many years of distance between us—only Christ could bridge the gap. Once I realized that, I became an active agent of reconciliation. The first step was being willing to let go, to relinquish my right to remember. To forgive.

Relinquish your right to hold onto past hurts. Forgive.

Reflection

How many people allow hurt, betrayal, or misunderstandings to separate them from the people they love? In speaking to people for over twenty years in ministry, I have often heard statements like, "He hurt me! I will forgive him, but I will never forget what he did!" And according to their words, they allow the offense to lurk in the crevices of their heart for years. But it doesn't have to be. I have also met others who found the grace to reconcile with jealous sisters, mean co-workers and even cheating spouses. Upon reflection, some described the past situation as laughable, and the memory reduced to, "I don't remember what she did — but I was so mad at her!" Some remember. But the individuals who release it forget.

There are, however, offenses that some will never forget like rape, brutality, or violent crimes. Such life-altering offenses are hard to forget. There is a lot of evil in this world, and people who allow themselves to be used to exact it. Sometimes it seems that life itself delivers fatal blows, causing us to ask, "Why me?" Two paltry words that can halt the process of healing altogether. But even in these cruel situations, when love prevails, reconciliation is possible.

I like Victor Hugo's *Les Miserables*. It tells the story of Jean Val Jean, an ex-convict who served a 19-year prison sentence for stealing a loaf of bread and trying to break out of prison several times. Finally paroled after several refusals, he receives refuge from a clergyman. Jean returned the favor by stealing his host's silverware. But the unexpected happens; once captured and brought to face the deed and the offended host, the bishop told the inspector that the silver was his gift to Val Jean. He forgave the deed and facilitated Val Jean's release. This single act of forgiveness from a total stranger became pivotal in Val Jean's life. For once, he had received and understood forgiveness and genuine love. He saw mercy in action. And that taught him more than he learned during his 19 years in the penal system. From that point on, Val Jean was a changed man. The rest of the story chronicles his efforts to build his reputation as an upstanding citizen. He gave his life and virtue to a downtrodden prostitute who later dies, leaving Val Jean to raise her daughter, Cosette—which he does until she becomes a woman.

Many questions could have stunted his progress and left him bitter—19 years for a loaf of bread—where was the equity in such a sentence! But rather than focusing on the wrong side of life, he was overcome by love. The scale had tipped in his favor. Love covered his sin, and that ruled the rest of his life.

When forgiveness and love prevail over bitterness and resentment, so will reconciliation.

Charlotte's Story Continued: Love Amidst the Mess-ups

During my 18-month layoff, I thought the pastor was teaching and preaching just to me. Every message I heard made me examine myself even further. But something else was happening during that time. God made special arrangements for the mothers of the church to mentor me. Spending time with them while I was fasting and praying, helped me to learn some vital lessons about taking the focus off me and putting it where it belonged; on God and helping others. My prayer was, "Less of me and more of thee!" He was making me to "lie down in green pastures" as the psalmist so eloquently penned. As a caring father, he was loving me and helping me to change. Experiencing His love like that, during a time when I felt my life and relationships were such a mess, helped me to trust Him. It taught me something else, too; if God could love me "just as I am," I didn't have to worry about seeking other's approval. "I'm okay in the skin I'm in!" A new, real, and down-to-earth me emerged.

In 2003, after reconciling with my sister, the Lord blessed me with a new job. My sister got married. She had her first child, and we started talking more freely than ever before. She even felt comfortable enough to talk about her own feelings concerning our relationship. I am so thankful. My sister has rededicated her life to Christ, joining a church with mothers who give her wise counsel to help her with her new roles as wife and mother. And now my sister is also my friend.

The pudding-proof of the finished work of our reconciliation happened in three stages: (1) when she asked me to be the maid of honor at her wedding; (2) when she came to visit me and took me to an Israel Houghton concert; and (3) when she got baptized in the name of Jesus Christ at Reconciliation Word Ministry — my home church in Royal Oak, MI.

I give God the glory for showing me, me. I glorify Him for reconciling me to Himself and for giving me the sister-friend relationship I always wanted. Together we are forging lasting, significant memories for which I always longed. I glorify God for reconciling my sister to Himself through the remission of sins and good conscience toward God, which comes from the baptism in His name (1 Peter 3:21). When I humbled myself, God answered my prayers and others reaped the benefits of my submission. The ripple effect goes on and on.

My sister and brother-in-law remain Deacon and Deaconess in their congregation. They also sing on the praise team and work on the sound crew. God is so good; they believe that God is preparing them for pastoral ministry sometime in the future.

The Lord has truly done exceeding abundantly above what I could have asked or imagined! There are many other testimonies from the great storm that turned my life upside down. Because God answered all of my prayer requests, I can now say my world is right-side up again!

Pearls From Charlotte's Story:

o **Have the courage to be vulnerable, expecting love to prevail.**

o **Become an intercessor—pray for others.**

o **Examine yourself.**

o **Seek God's approval above all others.**

o **Relinquish your right to remember hurts. Let it go.**

o **When forgiveness and love prevail over bitterness and resentment, so will reconciliation.**

One-Flesh Reconciliation
Asalei's Story

I wasn't much of a reconciler before I met Jesus Christ. I would write you off and go on my way without a backward glance. From my perspective, people had irksome and annoying habits, and I couldn't even stand my own mess! So when Michael and I married on April Fool's Day (my idea), I said, "I know we won't stay married, so this way we can just say, 'April Fool!' and not have to pay for a divorce." And I wasn't joking!

In my family community, all I saw while growing up were divorced, separated, or married couples who stayed "together" but seemed miserable. My expectations were low, and that set the tone for my reality. Our marriage was as tumultuous as our two years of shacking (AKA living in sin!). There seemed to be no low to which we would not sink to hurt each other. Why? Who knows? Growing up, we both had dysfunctional families. There was alcoholism, and unbelievers (on his side), and backsliding believers on my side. There was rampant adultery on both sides. To put the exclamation point on it all, the man I chose, Michael, had enlisted in the Marines at age 17 and gone to the Vietnam War, returning with Post Traumatic Stress Disorder (PTSD) and drug addictions.

So much worked against us. But the actual problem was that neither of us had a relationship with Jesus Christ. He believed in God, praying even while in the military.

But I had seen a lot at my mother's church that left me wondering if there was a God. So my actions followed my doubt. Not going into details, I was a hot mess!

Many years later, I realized that despite having everything I'd desired, nothing satisfied me. I had the handsome and hardworking husband—but he was also a hot mess. We had two children—a girl and a boy just as planned. Success? I landed the ideal career I had dreamed of since age five, and I lived in a two-story house with two cars in the driveway. My life looked great on the outside, but I still felt empty inside. *For what shall it profit a man, if he shall gain the whole world, and lose his own soul? (Mark 8:36)*

One day, home alone, I said aloud, "Jesus, if you're real, I'm ready." And from that moment, I have never doubted that He is real, and everything the Holy Bible says about Him is Truth! I started to change. But my husband—he remained the same, Michael. We went to church, but after four years, he just couldn't seem to stop sinning even when he responded to altar calls.

I forgave him when he spent all of his money on crack cocaine. I forgave him when he stayed out all night and didn't return my car, leaving me to walk through two feet of snow to take the bus to work. I even let it go when our son had to walk home several miles from sports practice in the cold. Oh my! I still get angry when I think about THAT!

No one could understand why I would not divorce him, including my teenage children. What happened on our 20th anniversary was the last straw. Michael handed me a gift as he headed out the door. It was a plastic key chain from the dollar store. I think I was in shock. I don't remember what I said. But I know that I did not rebuke him—I was just too stunned to process it. What I remember is thinking, "Okay, if this is what you think of me, that's it!"

What came to mind was the scripture that had given me strength:

Likewise, ye wives, be in subjection to your own husbands; that, if any obey not the word, they also may without the word be won by the conversation of the wives; While they behold your chaste conversation coupled with fear. Whose adorning let it not be that outward adorning of plaiting the hair, and of wearing of gold, or of putting on of apparel; But let it be the hidden man of the heart, in that which is not corruptible, even the ornament of a meek and quiet spirit, which is in the sight of God of great price. For after this manner in the old time the holy women also, who trusted in God, adorned themselves, being in subjection unto their own husbands: Even as Sara obeyed Abraham, calling him lord: whose daughters ye are, as long as ye do well, and are not afraid with any amazement (1 Peter 3:1-6).

At that moment, I repented and determined to dwell only on the positive side of Michael. At least he had thought to get me something! It had been a long time since he had given me anything on our anniversary. And at least the keychain was in the shape of a heart with the inscription, "Prayer Changes Things." That had to mean something—didn't it? So once again, I forgave.

Reflection

One of the most daunting challenges during the early days of marriage was filtering negative versus positive stimulus. I had a real "Aha" moment when I realized how concurrently the two flow together. Sometimes you get a little negativity thrown in with the positive, and vice versa. Relationships are like people; we are a dichotomy, a mixture of strength and weakness, light and darkness, bad and good. I eventually learned that our commitment at the altar was the seal that added that "sticky" factor, making it hard to walk away when times got hard. It became clearer that I would have plenty of opportunities to experience my husband in almost every situation possible. I thought I knew him well! We loved each other, but we still had to learn each other in close quarters. That would come as we experienced life together. I would witness aspects of my friend, my husband, that I never knew existed. As friends, I didn't see him experience financial hardship. I never saw him lose his temper or face a major disappointment. But I would witness every one of those aspects throughout the life together as husband and wife.

Together we faced a major health concern during my first pregnancy. I was hospitalized for an entire week because

I lost 25 pounds during the first trimester. Then at delivery, I had a cesarean section which resulted in another five days in the hospital. These crises and roadblocks allowed us to learn different things about each other. As life partners, we knew we were obligated to each other. That meant loving, encouraging, and serving our new family together. But it also meant weathering storms that would inevitably help to prune us and make us a healthier couple. It's just not possible to know what this feels like when you're at the altar, wearing fantasy apparel, complimented by rose-colored glasses.

It was also during my first few years of marriage, while I was getting to know my spouse, that I met other young married women who had no problem voicing their marital discontent.

I listened to them vent and complain about their husband's shortcomings. It caught me off guard because I had never heard my mother complain about my dad. And I didn't know too many young married couples. Before long, I found myself irritated by every mistake or shortcoming I recognized in my husband. His flaws became the big picture, though he had many great qualities. What saved me was my relationship with Christ. It was His slight whisper that awakened me to the device of deception that was being used against my marriage: "Don't bring the sorrow and discontentment of others into your household. Get your joy back and rejoice with your husband!" My eyes became opened. And the people who got cut off were those with negative words—not my husband! I realized how much Satan hates marriage and family and will use any device possible to destroy what God has put together. From that day forth, I determined to focus on the good, to be very discriminating regarding friendships, and to be thankful for my blessings. And my home became a haven of joy once more.

Asalei's Story Continued

My secret reconciliation had nothing to do with my husband's actions but everything to do with how much I wanted to please my Heavenly Father. Despite it all, I forgave. That was almost 20 years ago.

Our marriage has endured a lot, but the miracles far outweigh the bad. Just to name two miracles in our lives: 1) God healed me from cancer! Years later, I remain cancer-free; and 2) Michael became a deacon in our local church! Today, we can both testify that we are over comers! God has blessed us with good health, void of addictions, and life-threatening illnesses. Now I can say that Michael strives to love me, but he strives to love God even more.

Reconciliation requires accepting the good and refusing the bad.

Pearls From Asalei's Story:

o Focus on the good more than the bad.

o Forgive.

o Invite Jesus into your relationship!

o Determine to have a relationship that pleases God.

o Study the Scriptures and live by them.

Self Righteous Me:
My Humbling Journey of Reconciliation
Blanch's Story

So near yet so far. These five words best describe my relationship with every significant person in my life—including God. I know that now. But for a long time, I did not. Thinking myself to be good and responsible in every area, I was the oldest of 13 children, five sisters, and seven brothers. I had always determined to be generous, truthful, and lawful. I enjoyed people and followed the golden rule in how I treated others. I knew it was wrong to lie. So I didn't—even though I left out a few details from time to time. I married at age 18 and had two children by the time I was 22. I took excellent care of my children, confessed my faults, and avoided hard liquor and cigarettes. Compared to others, I considered myself to be a saint.

My spiritual journey began when I was just 13. I went to church with a girlfriend and got baptized. Before long, I joined the choir and even sang on a local gospel radio broadcast, The Bristol Bryant Show, which aired on WJLB in Detroit. School was important to me, but not enough to continue to college. I just wanted my high school diploma, so I could get a job and help my parents with my brothers and sisters. Life was different then. Jobs were available, and you didn't need a college degree to get a job—just good work ethics.

My status of being a mother of two at age 22 changed when I had a third child at age 38. It's hard to believe that she is thirty-something now and my oldest almost 50! It's been a journey. And where I thought myself to be a saint, successful mother, and dutiful citizen, I have had plenty of time to test my status and self-proclaimed righteousness. Today I stand, almost 70, looking back like it all just happened yesterday.

It was years before I realized that I was ill-equipped to make godly choices. Though a believer, I did not know enough about the Bible to please God or be led by the Holy Spirit. I always considered myself to be "lucky." But now I know the difference between "luck" and "blessed!"

But let us go back to where it all began. It was 1965. I was 18 and graduating from high school. It was a monumental year: I got my diploma, a job, and a boyfriend! These all seemed like significant accomplishments. But being a teenager, I took a walk on the wild side, which resulted in a decision to get married. Both being the oldest of our siblings, my husband and I were responsible people, so things were beautiful—for the first couple of years. I did not understand that everything was about to change because while we were both used to responsibility, accountability was another subject. We were only 18. And we just didn't grasp the concept of "forever."

The first baby came. Everything was wonderful. But having the second child, we experienced the first actual test of our relationship. Neither of us could make excuses for our behavior. It was the evening of a family cookout. I can still smell the tantalizing aroma of the ribs on the grill as if it were yesterday. My memories of that day again color all my senses. The phone rang. I was preparing the meat, so in my haste to answer the phone, I didn't realize that I carried my knife into the house. I immediately recognized her voice. She was "that woman," the one who reminded me of the song, "It's Your Thang, Do What You Wanna Do!" She asked to speak to my husband. Did she know it was me—the wife? Today was not the day. It wasn't happening. And once she realized it, she spewed out details about my man and my bedroom that only I knew. Oh, she knew it was me. Before I knew it, I had hung up the phone and was going after my husband, who took off running when he saw the knife coming. He was running, and I was running—with a knife. And my family was running behind me. It had to be quite a picture. All I wanted from him was to hear a denial. But he couldn't reason that, seeing the knife!

But we were young, 22 to be exact. And we moved past that drama and a few other nasty incidents. In January 1972, we worked together to secure our first home. Our finances were stable, but our relationship was still struggling. Our children, despite it all, were thriving in school, receiving academic trophies and awards, and the opportunity to travel. We had no problem working together when it came to our children. We determined that they would have the best of everything.

My husband excelled in his career. And I knew that I too could pull my weight if I had to. We were a good financial team. But behind closed doors, we weren't good to, or for one another when it came to marriage. It was 1981. And everything came to a screeching halt; my husband, deciding to start a new life for himself, moved out.

After a time, we both seemed to accept the separation and talked again—becoming friends; married though still living apart. I thought I was managing okay until it hit me—depression. It was January 1982. Something struck a chord in me, and I reasoned that my husband's decision to "do his thing" freed me to do the same. I didn't know it, but I was becoming a bitter woman, fueled by instability and insecurity. I can't explain it, but that state of mind propelled me into doing things for which I had always judged others. And for the first time, I knew and acknowledged that I needed help.

One day I picked up the Bible. For so long, it had been nothing more than a pretty centerpiece of family history, gathering dust. My eyes fell on the book of Job. Of all places to begin my journey—reading about Job, a man who lost everything! His sons, daughters, cattle, even his property. Then his body became covered with boils. Job's afflictions seemed insurmountable. But rather than adding to my pain during my weeklong pity party, Job gave me hope and comfort. Job's journey is a testimony that good people go through bad things, sometimes for no reason at all. I could relate to his story. In my self-righteous thinking, I was a "good person," right?

Reflection: What is a "Good Person?"

People think they can determine what it means to be a "good person." How many express the opinion, "Deep down, most people have a good heart!" But the Bible reveals that this thinking is not valid:

Jeremiah 17:9
"The heart is deceitful above all things, and desperately wicked: who can know it?"
　　　It's not **the heart** that makes one good.

Matthew 7:21-22
"Not every one that saith unto me, Lord, Lord, shall enter into the kingdom of heaven; but he that doeth the will of my Father which is in heaven. Many will say to me in that day, Lord, Lord, have we not prophesied in thy name? and in thy name cast out devils? And in thy name done many wonderful works?"
　　　It's not **wonderful works** that make one good.

Psalm 36:2
*"For he flattereth himself in his **own eyes**, until his iniquity be found to be hateful."*

Proverbs 21:2
*"Every way of a man is right in his **own eyes**: but the Lord pondereth the hearts."*

Proverbs 16:2

*"All the ways of a man are clean in his **own eyes**; but the Lord weigheth the spirits."*

Proverbs 30:12

*"There is a generation that are pure in their **own eyes**, and yet is not washed from their filthiness."*

It's not how we see ourselves in our **own eyes** that makes us good.

Jesus addressed this issue in His conversation with the Rich Young Ruler. The story is in Matthew 19:16-17:

"And, behold, one came and said unto him, Good Master, what good thing shall I do, that I may have eternal life? And he said unto him, Why callest thou me good? There is none good but one, that is, God: but if thou wilt enter into life, keep the commandments."

Jesus quickly dispelled the erroneous belief that men are good! He corrected this youthful man; ***"There is none good but one, that is, God!"*** It's only when we keep God's commandments that we become eligible to enter into life! That youthful man was glad to hear this:

"The young man saith unto him, All these things have I kept from my youth up: what lack I yet? Jesus said unto him, If thou wilt be perfect, go and sell that thou hast, and give to the poor, and thou shalt have treasure in heaven: and come and follow me. But when the young man heard that saying, he

went away sorrowful: for he had great possessions" (Matthew 19: 20-22).

This passage reveals more about the rich young ruler; he was a man of faith, attended temple service, and he kept the law. His dialogue with Jesus revealed that he knew there was more to life, which prompted him to inquire: *"What must I do to inherit eternal life?"* He asked the right question of the right person and received the direct answer. Yet he went away sad. Why? Because he was not willing to pay the price for the blessing he sought. He was willing to keep the commandments as long as he could also keep his riches too! He was willing to DO GOOD but unwilling to follow the one who IS GOOD!

We may think we are "good," but only God knows our make up! He imparts that revelation to us as we experience life and interact with others. It's not what we do that makes us good. We can do good. But if we refuse to follow Jesus, we cannot be good. Living by our own definition of good will lead us into self-righteousness. However when we become followers of Jesus He becomes our righteousness!

Blanch's Story Continued

Something had to change. People say that. But what does it mean? The situation needs to change? Is it that other people need to change? Or do we just expect life to change? I was in trouble, and I needed help. I just wasn't sure how to get it. Then one evening it happened; my eyes saw life from an entirely different view. I'm still not sure I can explain what suddenly opened my eyes. I was having a phone conversation with my soon-to-be ex-husband on the phone. The one minute we were talking, then I had a strange "out of body" experience. It felt pleasant, peaceful, and free. Looking down through my own eyes, I could see myself sitting there on the phone. Like Superman, I could see right through the floor and ceiling of the room below; my children were enjoying their usual playtime on the stairs but then that radiant vision changed. It became a funeral scene—everyone was there except me. Was I dying? The bells were ringing. I honed in on the tones of the bells. It turned out to be the doorbell. I was coming back, and I don't know what happened. My husband was at the door. How could he be at my door and on the phone at the same time? It was confusing. What seemed like seconds was, in reality, much longer. My husband, perceiving that something was wrong with me, had long abandoned the phone call to get to me. It wasn't my imagination. He was ringing my doorbell. How long had I been out of it? At least long enough for him to drive 20 minutes to get to my house.

The next morning I got out of bed thankful that another supervisor covered for me at work. I knew something had changed within me. It was confusing. For some reason, when I came to myself, life looked different—as if I was seeing through someone else's eyes.

God Speaks Through Dreams and Visions

"For God speaketh once, yea twice, yet man perceiveth it not. In a dream, in a vision of the night, when deep sleep falleth upon men, in slumberings upon the bed; Then he openeth the ears of men, and sealeth their instruction, That he may withdraw man from his purpose, and hide pride from man. He keepeth back his soul from the pit, and his life from perishing by the sword" (Job 33:14-18).

The following month, February 1982, there was indeed a funeral. We gathered to say farewell to my father-in-law. Sitting in the church, basking in the pure yum of a piece of coconut-pineapple cake, I reflected on earlier invitations to church. There were many, usually brushed off with excuse after excuse. This time, however, I heard the reply escape through the sweetness of coconut that lingered on my tongue—"yes, we will be back."

No particular sermon or scripture comes to mind. Only the sweetness of that coconut cake and the peaceful contentment I felt sitting there. It beckoned me. And I realized that it was not the cake. It was the serenity of the surroundings. It was because I was there, in church. The next month I went back. And the fresh sermon that I heard was so penetrating that it almost gave me that déjà vu feeling. It opened my eyes. I heard the word, received the word, and this time, responded to it. They baptized me that day, along with my two children, in the name of the Lord Jesus Christ.

87

Then Peter said unto them, Repent, and be baptized every one of you in the name of Jesus Christ for the remission of sins, and ye shall receive the gift of the Holy Ghost (Acts 2:38).

That was March 14, 1982. And 14 days later, I received the Holy Ghost, with my children filled soon after. We received power, and that became the witness that drew my husband within just two weeks. Though we were going through a divorce, I invited him to church. To my surprise, he not only accepted my invitation but he was all in— he got baptized!

Then in April 1982, on my way to a child support hearing, the Holy Ghost was ministering and convicting me of my natural choices. I didn't desire to stay in the marriage. The Holy Ghost in my ear: "What if Jesus had come down from the cross—where would you be?" And at that moment, I realized that His Spirit was more powerful than my flesh. My thoughts were no longer my own. I felt convicted to forgive and compelled to drop the divorce proceedings. My husband also agreed to drop the divorce. What had happened? The Holy Ghost blindsided my flesh, trumped my wicked, self-righteous thinking, and gave us another chance despite ourselves.

In May 1982, my husband moved back home. We thought it was over, but now we were starting over. There was a lot of work ahead of us. But we knew that just as God had forgiven us, He would empower us to forgive each other and to rebuild trust. The enemies that once devastated us: adultery, mistrust, financial hardships were defeated. We were reconciled to God and to each other.

That reconciliation, however, was once again challenged. Shortly after we got back together, I learned that my husband had a child from a relationship he had during our separation. The child, a baby girl, was born the month after he moved back home in June 1982. I thank God for the Holy Ghost. The love of Christ constrained me to press forward with the commitment we had made to stay married and work through it.

Component of Reconciliation: Commitment

And because we were both willing to say, "Yes!" God added to our family. What seemed like another blow, losing a fallopian tube during an ectopic pregnancy turned into a miracle, for in 1985, at age 38, with only one fallopian tube, I gave birth to our third child. Little did I know that while God was blessing, the enemy was still coming against us. But the grace of God! My son was driving to the hospital to see his new baby sister when someone hit the passenger side of his car. Thank God our oldest daughter was with my husband—she would have been sitting on the passenger side of the vehicle! My son was fine; my daughter was unharmed, and our baby was beautiful. Once again, God raised up a standard against the enemy.

But there was yet another test we would need to pass. My husband's daughter, whom he loves dearly, endured an unthinkable loss when as a teenager, her mother died of cancer. She was still in high school with nowhere to go. When I tell you God's grace is great, and the power of forgiveness is unmatched, it's true. We brought my husband's daughter into our family and our home. And to God's glory, all four children are college graduates and continue to be fruitful in their career choices. Each one has a miraculous story to tell.

I am so thankful for the lessons I learned from the book of Job: endurance, forgiveness, but most importantly, trust. Just when it seemed life threw that fatal blow, the Lord stepped in and stopped peril in its tracks. God saved my marriage. He taught me to forgive. And He taught me that He can take your old failed life and give you a new successful life. Like Job, my life now doesn't look anything like it did during our family's early days. *"The Lord turned the captivity of Job when he prayed for his friends"* *(Job 42:10)*. My change started when I surrendered.

In my own eyes, I was righteous—that translates into "self-righteousness!" But God shed some light on me with His Word; my righteousness was as "filthy rags!" So I have learned that self-righteousness thrives on man-to-man comparisons. You can always find some person who is worse off or more sinful than you are. But when you compare yourself to the Word of God—that's when you see the truth. When you say, "Yes" to the Lord, you will make great strides in your reconciliation journey.

You may have relationships that seem irreconcilable. But I hope my testimony gives you hope for your future. God worked a miracle in my family and I am convinced that He can do that over and over for anyone who asks Him to. If Christ died for reconciliation, shouldn't we at least determine to live for it!

Reconciliation requires a "Yes!"

Pearls From Blanch's Story:

o **Learn to see yourself through God's eyes.**

o **The Holy Ghost will give your relationship a second chance.**

o **When you reconcile to God, He can reconcile your relationship.**

o **Never compare yourself to people—compare yourself to God's Word.**

o **Be willing to say, "Yes!"**

The Day I Stopped Running
Toni's Story

It was the fall of 2005. Our women's ministry was returning from Juanita Bynum's Threshing Floor conference in Atlanta. Though I was saved for just two years, I felt like I had it all together, I was on such a spiritual high. I finally had the right man in my life—Jesus Christ. But little did I know that I was still under the powerful influence of my own fleshly choices. Yes, Jesus was with me and in me. But I still didn't get it—He would not force me to live for Him. I had to decide for myself. Before I knew it, I gave in to my flesh and resumed making the wrong choices for my life.

It started as an exciting, happy experience confirmed by Proverbs 18:22, *"Whoso findeth a wife findeth a good thing, and obtaineth favour of the Lord."* Resting on one of the ten scriptures I knew by heart, I was sure that I was "a good thing" and was found by the right man. But he was not the right man, and I was not his wife. The relationship turned out to be nothing but yet another distraction from my relationship with the Lord. I was doing things with this man, contrary to scripture, living like a sinful woman. Looking back, I can see what happened; I became fascinated, even swept off my feet by being spoiled with gifts. No one treated me that way before. Being an overweight woman, I lacked confidence, which caused me to make poor decisions. I became more broken down by my dating behavior. I traded holiness and my dignity to keep a man—something far less than what Jesus had for me.

The relationship went on a downward spiral, and I saw my "dream man's" true colors. He wasn't my promise from God, and I had become less than anybody's "good thing." He became angry, punching holes in the wall, swearing at me, even putting me out of the car. His anger was even worse when I denied him sex. He mistreated me, but I just didn't think I could do better, so I allowed him to treat me that way. There were so many signs he didn't love me. He never made time for me on holidays or came around my family. Looking back, in our almost four-year relationship, we were never together on a major holiday—not even for Christmas! Yet I stayed, still intrigued that this really attractive man, who was out of my league, gave me the time of day. I was in love. The truth was, I should have been out of his league! I was a saved woman and my father was the King! But what kept going through my mind was, "Not too many guys want to be with a big girl." But I was more than just a "big girl." I was God's girl. Instead of listening to my Father and being obedient to His word, I allowed an abusive man to tell me what to do, refusing to let me into his world or even wanting to be a part of mine. He never came to church with me.

The blessing that put a dent in the stronghold— I went back to church. And each time I went back, I got more and more of God's word in me until I had the strength to let that man go! One particular sermon the pastor preached hit home: "Get your house in order. Get rid of the toxic things in your life." Wow! Toxic. All I could see was that man's "toxic" face. But I was so hooked that I dismissed thoughts of leaving him as soon as they came. I didn't know how to do it. Another minister prophesied to me, "You don't owe people any explanations." I knew what God was telling me, "Just walk away." But I didn't. I continued to vacillate between right and wrong.

My church family did not give up on me. The saints were faithful in calling me, telling me how much they loved and missed me, extending their endless warm hugs whenever I went to church. But they just didn't understand what I was going through. And I didn't tell them. Everyone said they loved me and it energized me. But that man—his love was getting old, and I was getting tired—of him. I felt like I was on an endless treadmill with no off switch. I knew the real deal, but reality didn't shake me.

God gave me a dream:
I was in my apartment talking to my friend, nestled on the fire escape outside my bedroom window. A man came into my bedroom and got into my bed, fully clothed—something I would never allow! But he refused to get out. I left the bedroom and went into the living room to ask my family to help me get rid of this intruder. No one would help me. Then he entered the living room. We had a terrible argument that turned into a fight. He stabbed me. I could feel the blood running down my side then spilling onto the floor. As it hit the floor, the blood

turned into water. So much water, the man was drowning and I was trying to save him. But how could I? I couldn't swim either. Somehow the drowning-and-rescue scene segued into me running through the church doors screaming, "Help me!" But no one did. The man appeared and grabbed me right there in the church, and in my mind, I thought, "I'm dead!" God's Word was my only weapon. So I opened my mouth and quoted scripture. The more I spoke, the smaller he became—smaller and smaller, until he disappeared.

Reflection

A great enormous gun! That's one of the first things you visualize whenever someone mentions the word "weapon." Knives, machine guns, bombs, missiles, these are modern weapons used to wage war against the enemy. But when a Christian hears the word weapon, what should come to mind are weapons used to gain power over spiritual foes—not natural ones! Paul explained it like this: *For the weapons of our warfare are not carnal, but mighty through God to the pulling down of strongholds* (2 Corinthians 10:4). A gun is a tangible weapon, created to kill flesh and blood. People use firearms to destroy bastions, which can be institutions, places, or people defending or upholding principles or activities--like those used during World War II and the Korean War. But we, the people of God, are engaged in unique warfare. Our battles are not over matters of state, foreign lands, or earthly governments but rather spiritual realms. This war is waged between Heaven and hell, between Satan's doomed evil forces versus God's eternal, victorious forces of life. The fallen creature, Lucifer, wants revenge on God for having his heavenly revolt thwarted by the Almighty. For when he lifted himself up with pride, God cast him out of Heaven!

Since that fateful day, humankind, God's greatest creation has been under attack by Satan. And in earthen vessels no less! But he has waged a war that he cannot and will not win! *"For though we walk in the flesh, we do not war after the flesh: (For the weapons of our warfare are not carnal, but mighty through God to the pulling down of strong holds;)"* (2 Corinthians 10:3-4). Yes, God's people face strongholds! But we are equipped to pull them down!

Toni's Story Continued

Awakening from the shock of my surreal life-like assault, I could still feel the blood streaming. But there was no blood, and neither was there a man in my bed. I was not in church, but at home, having a nightmare from which I had to recover. God was shaking me—telling me to get my act together, that the man, who I thought to be the love of my life, was the source of significant harm. My defense was God's word. I didn't need a sage to interpret the dream, but neither did I have the wisdom to heed it. The dream shook me, but not enough for me to repent or change. I felt trapped in a mess with no way out. I was down and out.

It was Consecration, the perfect time for me to fast and pray with my church. I knew the routine; everyone turns off television and radio and fasts for so many days. Consecration was a time of purging the world and filling up with prayer. We read our Bibles and came to the temple daily for a solemn assembly. The period of consecration would culminate with a communion service where we would take wine and bread—together on the floor around the altar. Consecration was always a blessed time of cleansing our flesh, heart, and spirit. I really needed it.

My sister asked: "Are you going to take part in the Consecration?" After everything I had been through— my hurt, my pain, the abuse, my heart-shattering dream—I knew God was giving me a second chance. I knew what my answer should be, a resounding, "Yes!" But what I heard escape my lips was a flat "No." Communion service came and went that Friday night. I missed it. Saturday came, the day after the weeklong cleansing and service with blood and wine. Everyone was so light-hearted and free. And there I was. Bound. The next day would be Sunday. And I would stay home again. I could hear my sister and friends getting ready for church at 6:30 a.m. They came to awaken me. "Get up and put your clothes on. Let's go to church." But I had decided, "No, I'm not going." I thought they heard me, but someone called for me again at 7:00 and 7:30, "Get up, time to go to church." I laid there. About 20 minutes later, my sister's voice intruded my space, "You can bring Latonia to church, she's still getting dressed."

Then I heard the door close, and she was gone. They had left our friend with me, expecting me to bring her to church. She was already half-dressed. What nerve! They obligated me. I was so mad and determined to just drop her off and keep going. That would fix them. But where the dream didn't shake me, God gave me friends.

Reflection: A True Friend

Everyone needs friends, but not everyone has TRUE friends! The dictionary defines a friend, as "a person whom one knows and with whom one has a bond of mutual affection." But in today's society, friends are people in cyberspace, on your social media list—people who don't know you at all! They look at your pictures and read your posts, but for knowing the real you—they live somewhere on the other side of a keyboard and never get close to the real you. Proverbs 18:24 refers to a friend who sticks closer than a brother. And if you have siblings, you know they are born into your life, not chosen.

Growing up with sisters and brothers can be challenging, but also rewarding. Because you live in the same house from birth, you know that these are the people who will always be there. In your space—in good times and bad. You play together, get into mischief together. Love. Laugh. Fight. But at the end of the day, you know your sibling will always be an intricate part of your life.

How much more then is the friend who sticks closer than a brother! Nothing weak, fleeting, or disingenuous about it! A true friend cares enough to tell you the truth—even if you don't like it. A real friend will stick by you even when they can't validate you. Rather than enable you to do wrong, they will allow you to be disabled just enough to hobble back and get life right.

Component of Reconciliation: Truth

Toni's Story Continued

I took my friend to church, but I didn't drop her off. I sat in the back. As the service went on, I could hear a small voice say, "When the altar call comes, go up there." And just as I had answered my sister that morning, I told that voice, "No!" Then the sermon was over. And as the minister proceeded with the altar call, where I had determined to stay seated in my shackles, my body betrayed me, and I watched my feet take me to the front of the church and straight to the altar. There I was walking towards the pulpit, feeling like everyone was looking at me. I was looking at me! My body took over, proceeding to lift my hands in surrender, and spilling out a river of tears. And I heard a voice say, "I just want to hug her." And as she hugged me and ministered to me, I felt like I wanted to die. I remember thinking no one knew or cared about the real me. The voice at the altar answered every unspoken thought that came to mind, things I was too broken to utter. "He sees you. You will not die. Those thoughts of suicide are a lie. He cares, and He misses you so very much!" Those reassuring words caused the dam to burst, and I cried and cried. But this time, my brokenness was producing healing and repentance. I was so sorry. I could hear myself saying that over and over for what seemed like hours on the altar. When I got up, all the heavy burdens I had been carrying for so long disappeared.

Casting all your care upon him; for he careth for you.
(1 Peter 5:7)

It was true! Jesus cared about me. And he had taken the time to show me the truth, to give me a dream, to send me friends, and an intercessor at the altar. After everything that transpired in my life, all the men that left me, including my Dad, I just knew that when I failed God, that He would leave me too. But He didn't. He was the only man who stayed with me, seeing what a mess I had become, loving me past my pain. Jesus took the time to show me how real love looks and feels. And He made good on His promise, "I will never leave thee, nor forsake thee" (Hebrews 13:5). I had run away from God, but He was always there, waiting for my return. And on that Sunday in 2009, I ran back to God, and we remain, to this day, reconciled.

Pearls From Toni's Story:

o Open your mouth and speak the word of God.

o God's word is a weapon—use it!

o He will send friends to help in times of need.

o God sees you—He cares!

o Repent! It lifts the heaviness of sin!

o Jesus' love is real—He won't leave you!

Secrets Revealed
Quinn's Story

I opened the car door and got in. What was I doing? This man was a stranger, yet here I sat, going on a two-hour journey with someone I barely knew. Going to meet people I never knew existed. And I wondered, why can't I just stay in this beautiful downtown Florida condo or better still, lay on South Beach instead? But it was too late; I had said yes and a perfect stranger sat in the driver's seat...

The drama unfolded when I was 14. I discovered that the father who raised me, whose last name I bore, my "daddy," was not my biological father. Instead, my father was someone else, with his own family, his own life, and I wasn't in it.

As far as I knew, I was the daughter of a well-known singing mom and a dad with unique financial prowess — he had financed our home as a door-to-door salesman. It wasn't always an easy life, but I felt at home with the simplicity of our "one-chapter-story." I had not entertained the prospect of becoming the subject of an unfolding drama — complete with all the components of a compelling story.

I was at the technology store, with dad's products in hand, doing what I always did. There it hit me, an unfamiliar voice speaking words that were incomprehensible and unexpected: "Who are your parents?" There was some mistake—these people thought they knew me. But I absolutely did not know them. They didn't look the least bit familiar. For the sake of anonymity, I will call my parents, Jim and Ann Doe. I told him who my parents were. "Brenda!" he proclaimed as he drew his wife in to the drama: "This is Darnell's daughter!" It confused me. It elated them. I had just told him my parents were Jim and Ann Doe! Why was he introducing me to his wife as the daughter of someone named Darnell? Disregarding my confusion, both he and his wife chimed in about how much I had grown and how pretty I was, rambling on about their disbelief in running into "Darnell's" oldest daughter. Not only were these people mistaken, but they must be crazy. "You have the wrong person!" My rebuttals were unconvincing and irrelevant. They were so excited, they never heard me. It was a strange encounter.

That evening, when I was alone with my mother, I told her what transpired that day. How I ran into some of her "old friends" at the technology store, and they mistook me for someone else. To be honest, I thought it was hilarious that two people could be so excited, not realizing they were so wrong! But I had to ask my mother, "Why did that man think I was the daughter of someone named Darnell?" Like me, she seemed puzzled, answering, "I don't know."

Sometime later, I can't remember if it was a few days or a few weeks. My mother and I went for a drive as the two of us frequently did, just to talk. But somewhere in our usual

104

experience, the conversation turned as she explained, "You have two fathers—Jim Doe and Darnell." Well, I knew that I was young, only 14, and still chaste. But I remembered something about the birds and the bees from sex education class; you only needed one man and one woman to make a baby. She couldn't have expected to tell me something like that and think I wouldn't ask questions! "Mom, I can't have two fathers! Who is my father? What do you mean?" My heart was racing as I prepared for words that could change my life forever.

My mother looked me dead in the eyes and said, "Darnell is your father." With four words, my entire world turned upside down. I cannot explain it, but there was a shift from that defining moment. It was like a flood that swept me away into unchartered water. The man that I had known all my life that I loved was not my father, my daddy. Tears ran down my face. My emotions and my tears were unexplainable. At first, I thought it was just because my dad wasn't my actual father. But then I got that empty feeling of hurt, pain, disappointment, anger, and everything else a child has when their father isn't a part of their life. It all came rushing over me at once. There had always been a man who loved and cared for me. But the man who bore me, my biological father, had left me. Why? Did he not want me? Did he not care? How dare he let me take another man's last name? Why didn't he fight to be a part of my life? Then, after all the questions, the conclusions came: He doesn't love me. He is not my father. I will NEVER call him dad.

The Bible teaches, "The glory of children are their fathers" (Proverbs 17:6). I felt as though I had lost my glory. But why? I had a father in my life. We were a family. He was my mom's husband and my dad, and he had been there for me since the beginning. But this recent revelation caused me to plummet into a state of hurt and pain that would last for seven years—right until I met this stranger, this "biological father."

The years passed but the void in my heart did not. I was 21. An adult, capable of making my own decisions and plotting the course for my life. That's when Darnell reached out to me. I'm sure my mother's hand was in it because Darnell didn't have my contact information. And I didn't know that she had his—but I didn't ask questions. It was entirely my choice to decide whether I would reciprocate his desire: to establish a relationship.

Reflection

What is a relationship? By definition, it is a connection between persons by blood or marriage. But building and maintaining a meaningful relationship takes much more than the ties that bind people together. Daytime television shows prove that people need and seek help with their relationships. Divorce Court, TV psychologists and family and friends who duke it out while the world watches has become the new normal; people struggle with relationships. When communication, kindness, and love fail, the cords that connect become broken. And what's penned on paper—meaningless. Birth certificates, marriage licenses, and other legal documents state facts. But only people can build sound family foundations. Each individual born into a family brings unique value and opportunity for meaningful interaction, growth, and development. Personality, intelligence, emotions, sense of humor all vary. Families experience life together. They share holidays and special events. They laugh together, cry together, and experience triumph and even tragedy together. When individuals miss these pivotal moments they can easily become estranged from the family.

There are so many components that form healthy relationships and strong families. The obvious ties that bind family members together are kinship and proximity. But a healthy family needs so much more than bloodlines and shared space. Here are just a few other essential family ingredients:

Diversity
The family is the first structure where people become exposed to diversity. Though genetic breeding is the same, each person is born with his unique personality, talents, and views.

Love
Most people think that love is nothing more than an intense feeling of deep affection, as found in any reliable dictionary. But the Bible reveals in John 4:24, *"God is a Spirit"* 1John 4:8 states, "God is Love." Therefore, if God is a Spirit, and God is Love, we can safely conclude, "Love is a Spirit!" We should never limit our love to only

what we feel. We should act in the spirit of love. That should include both our thoughts and behavior. Do loving things! Say loving things! In that sense, love then transforms from a noun into a verb! It should always be something that we do versus something that we have!

Respect
The definition of respect is deep admiration or regard for another. That requires exposure. Like love, respect should be more than something we have, but something we give as an offering to everyone in the household. The family is the school ground where we learn the first lessons on respect. Thus, the family becomes the school ground for learning how to treat people in society at large.

Communication
To many, communication is nothing more than the imparting or exchanging of information or views. But how often do we find that imparting one's thoughts is not as much of a problem as hearing someone express what they think or how they feel? Listening—now that's a skill! Have you ever conveyed a thought to someone and watched them zone out while you're talking? It seems more natural for people to concentrate on what they want to say next rather than on what you are saying now! Honest communication is not just conveying or exchanging. It is hearing, processing, and understanding. Communication should produce results!

Shared Experiences

When people share experiences, they create history together. Attending birthday parties, graduations, or anniversaries—these life events create memories that weave the story of time spent together. So does enduring life's storms, adversity, conflict, sickness, and hardship. Shared experiences include these. Authentic and meaningful relationships include both the good and the bad, the pleasant, and also the unpleasant circumstances of everyday life.

Laughter

Scripture does not say, "The family that laughs together, stays together!" But the principal is true. Laughter is like the glue that helps people stick together in good times and bad. Laughter gives us memories and acts as a medicine to a bleeding heart.

Support

One benefit of being in a family, is the support the members give to one another. Everyone experiences times of weakness and distress through the difficulties of life. When trials come, it's a blessing to have someone to help bear the load. Whether a sister or a loving father, everyone needs a friendly face, a shoulder to cry on, or just a listening ear. It's nice to know that you can mess up and still have someone who will love you and be there for you no matter what! The family produces the first experiences of loyalty and unconditional love.

My parents (my dad, who raised me) did not want Darnell in my life because of the way he left my mother. His subsequent return and proposal came too late; My dad, Jim Doe, the only man I called "Dad," had plans for my mother and me that did not include that Darnell guy! I believed the account of this story—one marriage proposal came too late (Darnell), but the other was right on time (Jim Doe). On the day of our first meeting, the "D-man" sent several dozen roses and picked me up for lunch. We went to a restaurant near my job. I thought he was just doing it to make himself feel better for not being in my life all those years. I didn't know his actual feelings or motives, but my hurting heart refused to entertain that he could be sincere.

D-man was living in Florida but made frequent trips to Detroit on work assignments. During this first year, we saw each other many times during his business trips to Detroit. However, whenever I saw him, there were always other people around, including my mother. So our conversation was never personal, but more about this new family tree that was unfolding in my life. I learned that my grandmother had died; I met my grandfather, my uncle, aunt, and cousins. During these initial meetings, I also learned about my siblings, one older brother, two younger, and a sister. I felt disconnected all over again. It was not just a father I didn't know about, but an entire family! I discovered that my older brother lived near me in the Detroit area. He was there the entire time and I didn't have a clue. Our meeting was a pleasant surprise. Feeling like we were never strangers, I loved him instantly. He later moved out west. My younger siblings, however, lived in Florida, so I didn't meet them that year.

When D-man stopped working in Detroit, he went back to Florida, and he rarely ever called. I did not see him again for years! He facilitated a meeting for us in 2011 when I told him I was trying to organize a Florida vacation with friends. I guess he saw it as an opportunity to reach out. Again, I don't know how he knew this, but I followed my usual model to maintain peace of mind, "Don't ask!" After making just a few calls, D-man secured a condo for my friends and me for an entire week's stay! That was great news. But there was a catch: he wanted me to come a few days earlier than my friends so I could spend time with him and meet his family—my other family. To my surprise, I was excited about meeting my younger brother and sister. I was, however, nervous about being alone in the car with this unknown "daddy" for the two-hour ride it would take to get there. We had not spoken in over two years.

So here I sat—in the car with a man I hardly knew, going to a place I had never been, to meet people I never knew existed. As we drove, we talked about many things, nothing in particular. The ride was tolerable. We got to his house, a beautiful ranch and I met them, my little sister, my little brother, and my father's wife. The love I felt for them was a pleasant surprise. And the same way I am attached to my six (yes, I said six), brothers and sisters at home, I became attached to them. One meeting was all it took. I fell in love with his sweet wife and had a wonderful time with them. That was the day I forgave D-man for his absence. But I had a fight in my mind, comparing the hardships of my childhood--the cold nights with no heat—to the affluent life D-man provided his new family. He lived by the Ocean with his Hispanic wife, and his two mixed kids, driving a luxury car. I am laughing now because this thought was ridiculous. They didn't have a perfect life or anything, but for a moment I felt: "How dare he leave me to struggle like that!" But I had to let it go. And for a moment I did, seeing the tears in my little brother's eyes as I prepared to leave them. That connected feeling, left me hoping from now on, everything would be all right.

But all was not well. Though I had a good experience and fell in love with my siblings, I realized later that I did not forgive Darnell, my father, as I had thought. My heart ached.

I had another life-changing experience in 2011; on October 9, 2011, I was baptized in the name of the Lord Jesus Christ and filled with the gift of the Holy Ghost. This experience caught me by surprise.

The Holy Ghost revealed a lot of things to me in the next year, mostly about myself. Having Him in my heart truly changed me, and I witnessed the fruit of my transformation that following year when I had another opportunity to visit with D-man and my sister. This time they came to Michigan. It would be the first time they would see me as a new creature in Christ. And God was true to His word; old things passed away. And I beheld all things new in our relationship as I realized that the hurt I felt was gone! It was that moment that I knew God's Spirit had done an inward operation of complete forgiveness in my heart. I experienced the power of reconciliation! And I heard the words pouring from my lips: "I forgive you."

And not only that, but I could disclose all of my feelings. The Lord took me full circle to pure understanding, contrition and healing. I was no longer hurting but had gained a genuine love for Darnell. My biological father was back in my life by his choice and mine. Looking back, I can see that it was also by my Heavenly Father's choice as well.

Darnell might not have been a part of my life growing up, but God had a plan for me the whole time. The Word says, *"When my father and my mother forsake me, then the LORD will take me up" (Psalm 27:10).* I recognized that I had so much favor in my life. When things went wrong, somehow, I have always had provision and a sense of greater expectation. My earthly father may have forsaken me, but I discovered that I had a heavenly Father who had always been there and would never leave me! He is none other than the King of Kings and the Lord of Lords! How amazing is that? God blessed me so much that I just couldn't hold onto anger! I realized that God had a plan for me but He had one for Darnell too. Everything was working together for good! There was no more doubt, no more hurt, no more pain.

Component of Reconciliation: Let it go!

No one enjoys learning that their life is full of secrets! That's a hard truth-pill to swallow. It's also difficult to face unexpected adversity, even when it's with people you love and trust. But I realize that I wouldn't be the person I am today if I had not gone through the trials I went through growing up. I believe God was there for me the whole time, since I started seeking Him as a child. As the Scripture says, the Lord did "take me up," making a way for me when there was no way. It was God who helped me get through college. When I thought I was doing everything by myself, He was there. He never let me get too far away from him. As a child, I could hear His audible voice, these turned to visions as I got older. Now I can see that God always had a plan for my life! And even though I didn't know the full truth, I always knew that my life was important and I wanted God in it. I wanted Him to fill in the blanks. God chose me at a young age, and I am called to serve Him. He has been speaking to me my entire life. I ran from His calling from the time I graduated high school and throughout college. But I always knew where I was headed—right back to Him. He told me He would never let me go! And when I asked, and sought him, with all my heart—when I decided that I wanted all of Him, He led me to a fullness greater than I ever imagined possible. I know that even more is coming! Hallelujah! God had angels around me, leading me to where I needed to be, guiding me through the Scriptures, showing me His baptism, and sending me to a pastor who would feed me! I thank God for Reconciliation Word Ministry International! And now I am living proof that God's desire for us is reconciliation—to Him and others!

Yes, Jesus had a full plan for me before the foundation of the world, and before I was born. The road I traveled to get there was steep, it humbled me. But it positioned me to receive all that He had for me. I went through everything for a reason, and not all for myself, but to help others see His light in their darkness. Just as He revealed His plan for me, He could do the same for others.

I have become an intercessor, often praying for my biological father, his wife, and my sister and brothers in Florida and across the country. Whenever I pray for my family in Michigan, I am praying for them too. I desire to see my entire family saved. Maybe one day, Jesus will send me to them to lead them to salvation the way He led me.

The joy of the Lord is my strength, and he gives me peace that passes all understanding. He allowed me to let go of the pain and unforgiveness I had been holding onto for so long. Jesus is amazing, and I give all glory to Him for giving me the strength to forgive, and facilitating true reconciliation between Darnell and me. As for God, His way is perfect. The word of the LORD is tried and true! He is a buckler to all those that trust in him. Amen.

Pearls From Quinn's Story:

o   Life is a drama full of surprises.

o   Sometimes love comes from unexpected places.

o   God has a plan for your life.

o   God's love transforms the heart.

o   God wants us to be reconciled to Him and to others.

o   Through Jesus, you can let go of pain and forgive.

Let The Redeemed of the Lord Say So!
Lynette's Story

Over the past few years, I have found myself in the dark concerning my job. Notice the word used "job," not a career. Lending to these bleak feelings were several questions and doubts concerning my knowledge, growth, development, competency, and even my potential. This feeling was foreign to me. I had always been so thankful to God for what I thought was excellent preparation, a graduate degree, and blessed opportunities. But now I had questions: "What's missing now?" and "What am I doing wrong?" I just felt like the forward motion in my job path had come to a screeching halt. I was in a stagnant place.

The only thing that kept me going through this was something I had learned about God; He operates in seasons. And these require alignment with His Word and obedience. This story tells how God positioned me for change and to receive the blessings He has prepared for me.

It all started about six years ago when my job was ending. My company offered me a separation package that also required me to secure another position within three to six months. It happened so suddenly all I could ask God was, "Wow, Lord, what am I going to do now?" I was the sole supporter of an adolescent son, still in grade school, a house, and bills—so much responsibility. God was my sole support system. It was all in His hands.

Let your conversation be without covetousness; and be content with such things as ye have: for he hath said, I will never leave thee, nor forsake thee.
Hebrews 13:5

I was getting closer to the terms of my separation package. The reality hit me: no job! I just couldn't believe that God would forsake me. Looking to Him once more, I remembered an internal position I had applied for earlier. I didn't realize it then, but in retrospect, I know that it was God who directed me to contact the department manager (since she never contacted me). I was able to find my initial email to her and sent a follow-up note, "I'm still interested in working for you. I would greatly appreciate the chance to interview for an open position in your department." Shortly after, I received an email response. Delightful news—she accepted my request and granted me an interview for a Supply Chain Analyst position. I got the job! Just like that! Wow!

I was so excited about starting this position and intrigued by my new manager, a successful African-American female in a highly technical field. I thought she had a lot going on and so much more to offer me as an eager new learner. She would make an excellent mentor who could contribute a lot to my career as I continued to become established in the business. What seemed to pose an impending threat to my job and livelihood had taken a surprising turn for the better. Things were looking up.

Continuing in the position for years, I soon noticed a gradual change in the corporate culture; managers were devalued and demoted, the workplace had become disarrayed—mismanaged. At that point, corporate transition into new management, which seemed to result in things getting back on track. In fact, during my annual review, I was asked, "Do you have a mentor?" I did not. But I was eager to have one to boost my growth and professional development. So I asked my boss if she would consider becoming mine. She was knowledgeable, progressive, and stylish—I admired her. I was excited and ready to learn. As the restructuring progressed, however, I realized that the mentorship arrangement fell short of what I expected. Hopes dashed, I questioned my relationship with my boss.

Still pressing forward, our department engaged in a new vehicle launch. It should have been an exciting time. All I could think about, however, was the lag in my own professional development. I just didn't have the support my mentor promised to enable me to reach my full potential. I requested meetings to discuss my progress and express my concerns. But each time I scheduled a meeting, she canceled it. I was so disappointed, I began to wonder about my future. Did she mean it, or did she just agree to mentor me to put a quick end to the review? I had so many questions and so little confidence in my boss. Our relationship became fractured. After much prayer, I began my search for a new job.

My work experience seemed to be on a steady decline, with no job prospects in view. It seemed the more I prayed, the worse things got, and it was becoming harder and harder to go to work each day. Beginning to lose my confidence, I knew I needed a change—and that would only come by God's grace. In all my complaining and disappointment, I lost sight of a very critical truth— God's grace is sufficient! His grace was there the whole time, right in the middle of my work situation. I had been focusing on the negative aspects of my circumstances without recognizing what God was doing for me. He was moving, guiding, and always giving me favor. I needed to choose Him again, to put Him first, and look to Him to be my mentor and role model. But to receive His guidance and hear His voice again, I needed to be set free. I needed to forgive.

It was hard to swallow; I had put a person in the place where only God should be, and resented her when she couldn't deliver. The truth—only God could ensure my growth and development, not my boss. I didn't know it then, but the whole situation was positioning me to learn to trust in Him. He used my boss, the circumstance of change, and, last, my sister. She told me to pray for healing, growth in my workplace, and the ability to forgive my boss. I knew that God was using my sister to confirm His instructions to me. I struggled with it. I felt like I was in a fight with myself: "Pray for her—No, I don't want to!" The bottom line was irrefutable; no obedience—no relief, no peace, no healing, and no victory.

So often people think the road to victory is glorious. But during this experience, I learned that success comes with a cost. There will be times that you have to humble yourself, submit to God and also to authority. Confess evil thinking, and yes, that victim mentality that complains instead of taking a proactive approach. Once I learned this, God started showing me—me. In my frustration, I had become angry and prideful, ungrateful and whiny, and distant from God. I experienced fear, pain, disappointment, neglect, guilt, and shame for the person I had become. And for the first time I realized that God had not left me; it was I who had left God. I wanted to run away, to quit my job so I could experience immediate relief from these feelings, my boss, and the pressure of interceding for a person I had grown to dislike. But I slid even deeper into the abyss. I began doing hateful things like ignoring my boss's emails, disregarding her instructions, or being compliant when I got around to it. I became lazy and argumentative, challenging her every word. But I didn't see this side of myself because I was so busy blaming my boss for forsaking me, for hindering my growth and putting up roadblocks to my professional development. When God showed me who I had become, it arrested me. I was in this resentful place because of my pride. Was it possible that I, Lynette, had turned into such an unlikeable, disagreeable, and ungodly woman? My behavior

121

exemplified nothing I had learned in Word Study or read in the Bible. I called myself "Christian," but I was not behaving "Christ-like." It was my moment of truth. I needed reconciliation both with God and my boss.

The prospect of reconciling was humbling but what I needed to do. My sister was right, I needed to pray for my manager and forgive her. It was the only way to get relief, peace, and healing. Yet I struggled to do it. I felt as if there were chains holding me in bondage. I needed God to liberate me. I didn't want to pray for her because I thought she was making my life miserable on purpose—the devil in living color! Something had to change. I had to change.

Component of Reconciliation: Self-examination

My first solid step towards reconciliation was self-examination. I came to grips with some hard truths about myself: I had given a person too much power over my success; I was acting out of bitterness—being disrespectful and insubordinate; I was harboring unforgiveness. These were hard truths to face. I was walking in fear, guilt, shame, and pride. According to the Bible, that was no way for a professing Christian to live. These were painful and disappointing revelations. I could see why so many avoid the process of self-examination. It's hard. It hurts. But I knew I could not move forward in my career, my spiritual development, or my relationship with God until I became free of this bondage. I had to walk it out. I had to let God correct me.

My next step was prayer. I prayed that I would walk in God's expectation. I prayed about my bad attitude and complaining. I prayed about the condition of my heart. This time whenever I had evil thoughts about my boss I prayed for her and that my wrong feelings would cease. Each and every day I entered into the building I prayed, reminding myself that as a Christian, I work for the Lord! I posted prayers in my cubicle regarding my attitude, speaking God's words, praying for cleansing. This was a battle I had to win. Defeat was not an option.

God was (and still is) dealing with me in more ways than one. As I faced the first steps toward reconciling, my feelings were all over the place. I experienced fear, pain, neglect, guilt, and shame. I was disappointed that I had let this grip me for so long. This was a substandard quality of life for a professing Christian. I didn't think so at first, but pride hindered me, and paralysis halted me. Why had I allowed myself to become so distant from God? I felt a tense, hot burning on the inside that I didn't like. The thoughts that followed were "just quit this job, you'll feel better." I knew this anger would subside. But did it? No, for my behavior toward my boss became spiteful, insubordinate, unprofessional, and sloppy. I challenged her every word. When God showed me the person I had become, I couldn't deny it. I was not the Lynette I used to be nor the child of God He called me to be. The Holy Spirit showed me—I had put my manager on the pedestal that belonged only to God. No wonder I was so disappointed. I don't know how or when it happened. All I could do was repent and ask God to forgive me and put my focus and my life back in order. My two-word prayer, "Yea, Lord."

I realized that saying, "Yes!" to God also meant saying, "No!" to Lynette. I wanted immediate resolve, and only God could do it! Several Bible passages came to mind — these helped lay the foundation for my new direction:

"But seek ye first the kingdom of God, and his righteousness; and all these things shall be added unto you." (Matthew 6:33)

"Create in me a clean heart, O God; and renew a right spirit within me.
Restore unto me the joy of thy salvation; and uphold me with thy free spirit."
"The sacrifices of God are a broken spirit: a broken and a contrite heart, O God, thou wilt not despise." (Psalms 51:10, 12, 17)

"Be still and know that I am God." (Psalms 46:10)

"But the Comforter, which is the Holy Ghost, whom the Father will send in my name, he shall teach you all things, and bring all things to your remembrance, whatsoever I have said unto you." (Psalms 14:26)

These are the primary scriptures that inspired me to be obedient and continue to press on as Jesus had pressed on for us. "Take Me to the King" is a song (amongst others) that sets the atmosphere of worship, allowing me to hear God and prepare for a breakthrough. My friends and family held me up and held me accountable. Many of them continue to support me in my growth process, especially my sister, who has been my most ardent and influential votary, encouraging me to forgive my boss and myself for past failures.

During this time of seeking, I also aligned myself with a Christian women's group whose focus was vision and goal planning. Adding their testimonies of action and success, along with the preaching and teaching I received at church, I was becoming more empowered. The weekly Word Studies were so timely, teaching us to read, speak, and do God's word— to declare the decree:

"I declare the decree according to God's Word, that He has not given me a spirit of fear, but of love, and power, and a sound mind—for His glory!"

The reconciliation encounter was inevitable. The perfect opportunity came when it was time for the department Performance Reviews, scheduled to be finished by the end of December. However my review was scheduled for mid-January. I was ready. I figured I could use this time to discuss growth and development, strengths and weaknesses, and mentorship. I wrote down points and questions from past reviews and the things I needed and expected from my manager. I was ready, but my manager was not; she canceled the performance review twice! I became angry all over again.

When the day finally arrived, I reported to Human Resources, positioning myself in the HR manager's office as instructed. I went in praying. My manager opened the discussion, identifying "performance met" categories. However, as she read the review, she also showed behavioral changes that she felt were not pleasing or meeting standards. I explained why, apologizing for being disrespectful. She accepted and continued listening. During the conversation, I didn't feel that she took responsibility for her mismanagement, lack of leadership, or the lack of mentoring to help individuals grow and develop. The meeting ended without resolution as she rushed off to another appointment. Her last comment was that if I needed to continue the conversation, I should set up another meeting with her. I shook my head in disbelief. She knew the review was incomplete, yet she ended it. And even though she failed to schedule a subsequent meeting to discuss my leadership concerns, I knew I had the victory; God gave me peace. I had confessed, repented, and prayed for my manager. And though nothing definitive ever came from my candid disclosure with my manager, I gained valuable insights into settling my wrong with God. He protected me from the attacks of the enemy long enough to regroup and shift my focus back on Him. God showed me His love, mercy, and grace, which endures forever.

In conclusion, I thank God for allowing me to examine my feelings and emotions and to receive healing from hurt and disappointment. I thank the Lord for never forsaking me and freeing my heart from bondage. I give God all the glory, honor, and praise! I was ready to quit, but God enabled me to continue. My situation felt impossible, but he gave me hope in the midst of it. He was my light in the darkness.

Now, God continues to walk with me in my career paths. He has taught me that reconciliation is not only for my relationship with Him, but everyone He places in my life. I know that He will fight every battle as I remain still, remembering that He is in control. God is who he says He is; the King of Kings, The Alpha and the Omega, the Beginning and the End. I hope this testimonial blesses and encourages the person reading it. God is real and able! Submit to Him even if those who oppose you don't! Put Him first in all that you do, and He will guide you and give you peace.

Pearls From Lynette's Story:

o **God is in control everywhere, even in the corporate setting.**

o **Self-examination will help you change even when your situation does not.**

o **Surround yourself with a godly and praying support system.**

o **Prioritize reconciling to God, and He will fight your battles.**

o **God will be your light in dark places.**

Reconciled To Eve
Portia Hewitt

Many regard the story of Adam and Eve as an unnecessary tragedy of epic proportions. Unnecessary because Eve made a wrong move when she disobeyed the instructions God gave to Adam—they were both forbidden to eat of the tree of knowledge of good and evil. Tragic because her action was the catalyst for the fallen state of all humankind. And epic because her action set the stage for the entire Bible and course of man's journey back to the right fellowship with God. Eve's actions exhibited the frailty, vulnerability, and flaws of the flesh. But what became most clear was that one person's disobedience could hinder the blessings of all people forever! There are benefits when we obey God and devastating consequences when we do not. Eve's deception and Adam's disobedience exacted eternal consequences on all of us:

1) Estrangement from the creator: God will not and cannot abide or fellowship with the darkness of sin and uncleanness.
2) Hard labor: God's judgment upon the man is that he will forever work by the sweat of his brow.
3) Female submission: God's judgment upon the woman is to submit to men.
4) Suffering and travail: the most blessed event of childbirth comes through pain and suffering.

Who would think that one act of disobedience could cause such calamity and dire consequences through every generation forever!

Traces of Eve remain in every woman arrested by her flesh, evil thinking, and frivolous hopes. Eve arises in a daughter who rebels against her mother. In a wife who takes the lead over her husband and household. And in a sister who imparts foolish advice, leading others astray. Yet, even with all of her flaws, God loved Eve. And it's that love that compels Him to continue writing our reconciliation story to this day.

I found Eve in women's ministry. As a Pastor's wife of a suburban church, I have seen Eve's curiosity of forbidden fruit often. It lures her into adultery, circles of discord, and figurative castration of her husband's manhood and headship—sometimes without him even recognizing it! I saw Eve taking charge of decision-making, leading her family, friends, and new members into the wilderness. Eve usurped authority over unsuspecting souls causing them to become scattered, vulnerable, uncovered by a shepherd assigned to teach and preach God's Word. I saw what I likened to an implosion. Leaving my purpose to aid, instruct and guide, void. In one sweeping moment, I felt that my survival depended on escaping Eve, lest I become broken. Like Eve, I found myself naked, estranged and removed from the beautiful place of joy, safety, and abundance. I felt powerless, though God had done so much to make me powerful. I felt guilty for failing both

130

God and unsuspecting women overcome by "Eve-Syndrome."

In church terms, this syndrome is akin to apostasy. An apostate is one who changes loyalties and aligns with oppositional forces, choosing self-will over the statutes of God's Word, yet maintaining the title "Christian." They have a form of God but deny the power thereof. The apostate woman rejects biblical principles and practices and even rails on the leaders who promote God-given standards—in favor of entering alliances with others who think and do the same. She appeals to the flesh and every deadly sin that flows from it—lust, pride, greed, rebellion, disobedience, discord, the list goes on.

Through the years, I have heard many identify Eve's crime as being deceived. She believed the lie Satan told to lure the new humans away from God: eat the forbidden fruit and be as gods! (Genesis 3:5) Deception is a masterful device. It means: *something intended to mislead somebody; it is the act of tricking, conning, and cheating someone out of something.* I am seeing deception as one of the most dangerous and dastardly weapons Satan uses to seduce and capture God's people. Other devices pale in comparison. A person knows when he steals or lies, or his flesh is gripped by lust. But the weapon of deception is so subtle and imperceptible that it catches its victims off guard. The deceived becomes "tricked," and "cheated!" Deception is so powerful that an individual does not know when it happens or that it happened! He becomes duped into believing that his thoughts and actions are right and all right with God! It becomes a mental, emotional, and spiritual stronghold that consumes an individual; it becomes a part of his daily operation in every thought, intention, and deed. The deception becomes a part of his identity; it is not what he does, but who he thinks he is—and there's "nothing wrong with it!" The surrounding factors set the stage for making choices that are not expedient or could lead to more troublesome vices. Cause and effect: "If I do this, what will I cultivate?" The concept: the fruit that grows in your garden is what you plant there!

The strength of deception lies within the deceiver. While a person is in the deceiver's presence, he is oblivious to its manipulation because the operation is subtle, even exciting to be around—it feels good. The elements of charm, charisma, fascination all come into play. The deception spreads like the sneezes of a cold or a contaminating physical touch. The deceiver at once finds himself surrounded by others who affirm his operation. A deceiver is often a person of great influence—someone who is well-liked. In fact, people want their approval and validation. What emerges is a community of flesh-led individuals who share in the same mindset: It just sounds right! It feels right! Therefore—it must be right! Could so many people be wrong? It's this camaraderie that adds fuel to the fire of deception; strength in numbers. One accord. My pastor often spoke about "silly women." He seemed so miffed, insulted, and perturbed that I often wondered why the topic was such a big deal. Now I see why! Just look at 2 Timothy 3:1-9:

*"This know also, that in the last days perilous times shall come. For men shall be lovers of their own selves, covetous, boasters, proud, blasphemers, disobedient to parents, unthankful, unholy, Without natural affection, trucebreakers, false accusers, incontinent, fierce, despisers of those that are good, Traitors, heady, highminded, lovers of pleasures more than lovers of God; Having a form of godliness, but denying the power thereof: from such turn away. **For of this sort are they which creep into houses, and lead captive <u>silly women</u> laden with sins, led away with divers lusts,** Ever learning, and never able to come to the knowledge of the truth. Now as Jannes and Jambres withstood Moses, so do these also resist the truth: men of corrupt minds, reprobate concerning the faith. But they shall proceed no further: for their folly shall be manifest unto all men, as theirs also was."*

This passage is very revealing. The opening describes perilous times in the last days. The epistle writer describes the mindset and operation of people in these times. They will love themselves, go after what others have, and speak highly of themselves. They will speak disrespectfully about God and holy matters. And they will, by nature, be disobedient and unthankful. In these perilous times, unnatural affection will be prevalent. People will make false accusations, even despise those who strive to walk uprightly before God. They will betray others, thinking themselves to be much more than

133

they are. By definition, the word "highminded" refers to people who have high moral standards, but in the Bible, the word means proud. And according to Scripture, this is one of the seven things God hates! Thus the phrase, "godly-proud" is an oxymoron because there is not one instance in the entire Bible where "proud" has a positive connotation—not even for God! He never told us to be proud, and He never said He is "proud of us!" God used the phrase "well pleased." The high-minded or proud woman favors her own rules over God's laws. James 4:6-7 reads: *"God resisteth the proud, but giveth grace unto the humble. Submit yourselves therefore to God. Resist the devil, and he will flee from you."* Proud people lack humility and submission to God which, according to James, comes from the devil! The proud person, the epistle writer describes, will also appear to be godly, having "a form of godliness." Don't be deceived. This person will look good on the outside, but will reject God's Word and the leading of the Holy Spirit. This proud, disobedient person walks and operates according to her own will. She is a lover of self and has the ability to recognize, target, and lead other silly women laden with sin. Silly women manifest who they are by their speech, clothing, attractions, pride, and resisting the Word rather than resisting the devil. The perilous times woman will spy out the camp and prey on the foolish, claiming authority.

The same thinking became the engine that drove men to build the tower of Babel in Genesis, chapter 11:1-9. After the flood, the Lord instructed Noah and his family to multiply and replenish the earth. Yet as they journeyed, they found a flat land and dwelt there and built a city. Next they desired to build a tower unto heaven and a name for themselves. *"And the Lord said, Behold, the people is one, and they have all one language; and this they begin to do: and now nothing will be restrained from them, which they have imagined to do" (Genesis 11:6).* This self-will, opposed God's instructions; they were to go forth and multiply to replenish the earth. And for this cause, God confounded their language that the people of the land would no longer speak the same language. No communication— no tower—no tower—no fame! The people scattered across the earth. God would have His way and the earth would be replenished as He intended. So much for carnal oppositions to the Most High God!

This lesson teaches us that following man only produces selfish and fleeting fame while following God blesses the whole earth and everyone in it. God immediately intervened because he knew the power of unity; they would have accomplished their selfish goal of building the tower and making a name for themselves. And the rest of the earth would have remained void of citizenship. What looked right to the people was bad for humanity and in direct opposition to God's will and purpose. This story illustrates that there is power in unity. But it also shows the devastation that results when people become unified behind an evil cause. Just because the majority agrees does not signify that the majority is right!

Here is another point about deception—it operates as a force of influence. At the root of it is ignorance; *"My people are destroyed for lack of knowledge" (Hosea 4:6).* At the heart of it is disobedience, even rebellion; *"Behold, to obey is better than sacrifice, and to hearken than the fat of rams. For rebellion is as the sin of witchcraft, and stubbornness is as iniquity and idolatry" (1Samuel 15:22-23).*

The revelation in these passages is that a deceived person does not realize that his actions can bring forth destruction. Neither does he know that his sin and stubbornness have united into a stronghold akin to witchcraft—an evil practice scholars identify as an "irresistible influence, attraction, or charm." The Scripture further defines stubbornness as bringing forth yet another spiritual crime—idolatry, which means: "excessive or blind adoration or devotion." It is plain and straightforward; whatever or whomever we put before God, His Word, and His instructions become that thing we serve and worship. Whatever thought, desire, object, or person made higher than God becomes our god. And once that seed takes root, a new master is in control. That control will continue until the deception is exposed, disrupted, or shaken!

What enables a person to escape the clutches of deception? According to the tower of Babel story, it takes God's divine intervention! In the story, God identified, disrupted, and disbanded the force of deception that led the people into their idolatrous pursuits. The weapon he used—confusion. God confounded their language. They lost their unity when they no longer spoke the same thing! This incident teaches a life-changing truth: the best remedy to dispel deception, rebellion, and idolatry is to pray for God to confuse the perpetrators and to disrupt their unity! I learned this the hard way. I tried pointing it out, teaching it out, even preaching it out. But I learned that the only way to dispel unified deception was to pray it out! And I watched as it crumbled before my eyes.

I witnessed God's masterful hand disintegrate the entire operation in a few short weeks. He lifted the stronghold, cleansing the atmosphere of every "high thing" that had exalted itself against His Word. Some people left, others repented; worship became free, and the Holy Ghost began to be poured out in numbers! We experienced mighty deliverance as His powerful blessings flowed through the few that remained. One returning visitor commented: "It feels so much better in here! There's something new going on with the women—what I felt during my first visit, I decided not to come back! But I'm glad I did!" No longer did I look for strength in numbers, but power through God's anointing. I continue to thank God for this essential lesson.

Eve's story and the Babel incident both showcase the divisive weapon of deception. Eve lived in paradise and heard the very voice of God. Yet she succumbed to the voice of a lesser creature that God made. This account shows how fickle people can be, but also how we can miss the warning signs when we hear something that appeals to our flesh. Oh yes, the message sounded tantalizing: "Ye shall be as gods!" And remember, that was Lucifer's downfall all along—he wanted to be like the Most High.

He wanted to plant that seed in us. Another lesson learned: know who is talking to you! It may sound good, but if the messenger is less than reputable, beware! A snake delivered the message to Eve! Once she acted on it, sin prevailed, and shame ensued. The deceiver's plan was working in full swing: he aimed to deceive God's creation into serving him instead—whether it was angels in Heaven or Mankind on Earth! He used his beauty and popularity with angels in Heaven and his cunning subtlety with people on the Earth. The device never matters to the devil, as long as he gets results!

The first seeds of the deception brought forth accusations:

"And the man said, The woman whom thou gavest to be with me, she gave me of the tree, and I did eat. And the Lord God said unto the woman, What is this that thou hast done? And the woman said, The serpent beguiled me, and I did eat." (Genesis 3:12-13)

Adam pointed his finger at Eve, and Eve pointed hers at the serpent. God discovered them from their guilty hiding place. With innocence gone, they learned that they could not hide the nakedness of sin with a few fig leaves. It was too late to retract the life-altering effects the deception and disobedience had forged within their very constitution. Eve was forever changed, and Eve passed those changes to us. Adam and Eve's deception and disobedience caused everyone to be *"born in sin and shapen in iniquity."* And like our progenitor, we too would need to become reconciled to God.

The Awakening

Lying awake in a hospital bed, realizing my state, I reflected on the spiral of events that had landed me there. For nine months prior, I was a Foster Care Case Manager, traveling across the state, driving three hours round trip to and from work each day, and managing very stressful court appearances. As I lay in that bed, I could still see the faces of my foster children, some with broken hearts, some with broken bodies, and others shattered from all kinds of abuse. I recalled the attorneys that befriended me while we waited for hearings only to throw me under the bus in court. I thought of parents who refused to stay sober long enough to get their children back. I thought of the massive reports I had produced and the even greater ones I still needed to write. I felt broken all over again.

It was there, in that unavoidable, vulnerable state that God whispered to me: "Are you going to let me be in control? Of your life, your family, your children, my ministry—my people!" Had I become Eve? Had I taken everything and everyone in my world into my own hands? Lying there, I realized the weights that were lying on my chest, resting on my shoulders, weighing in my heart; I bore it all. The yoke that was His alone to bear. I reflected on my 20-year journey in ministry, for during that time, I had pressed to mentor and train women who refused to conform to the Word, and even worse, who led other women into rebellion. I had personal desires but I put them on hold, placing other's needs ahead of my own. I thought I was doing the right things for the right reasons. But resentment had crept into my heart.

It was that resentment that pressed me to complete my college degree before I turned 50. I just knew God would enable me to do it with excellence—period. Getting that degree was critical to my sense of accomplishment and fulfillment of a lifelong dream. And it was that accomplishment that qualified me to become a caseworker. Getting that degree was my dream. I wanted to be a blessing to the people of God. But feeling rejected by church women, I pursued a job as a social worker.

God showed me the benefits of working a secular job for a brief period. It helped me to not only become more relevant, but it also enabled me to relate to God's daughters more. Gaining a BA in Family Life Education, boosted me to go out into society and become reacquainted with the lost, to be touched by their infirmities, removing the "church fence" I lived inside of for so many years. I wanted to be like Jesus, known as the friend of publicans and sinners. Isn't Jesus our High Priest, touched with the feelings of man's infirmities?

Once I snagged the social worker position, my journey began—again. I met women whose histories were void of any spiritual connection. Many had strongholds of all sorts of addictions. Others were victims of violence and abuse. There was generational poverty where several family members remained in the social welfare system. I saw angry and hopeless parents who blamed a system that sought to shield children from the problems they caused. There was plenty of blame to go around. I met abandoned children, who were abused, and broken. Men who were so beat up by life that the haunting, empty look in their eyes spoke more loudly to me than their words ever could. That was heartbreaking.

On the professional front, I experienced a system so full of apathy that hope was becoming a fading entity even for those assigned to aid. Beaten down people were everywhere, in the home and the state offices. Cynicism was all around me, and it was looking like a lost cause. There was a cycle of open wounds, lacerations, bandages, and resuscitation—repeatedly. State laws prohibited me from initiating any ministry. I knew, however, that there should be more than a handout. The best solution for turnaround was a hand-up and spiritual transformation.

After months and months of looking into the shell-shocked eyes of five-year-old victims, young addicted women, broken men, and disillusioned workers—after driving miles to unknown places to host meetings between estranged mothers, fathers, and children; after court hearings, home meetings, and massive reports; there I lie awake, in a hospital cage of affliction, left with nothing but pain and my thoughts. And I realized that what I had devoted my life to, was what I also needed—reconciliation.

At that critical moment, I saw myself. I needed to become whole, at peace, and acceptable to Jesus Christ once again. That was the moment I realized the bitter truth my pain had obscured— I controlled nothing. There was nothing in me that could change any situation I witnessed. I couldn't calm one storm, re-write one life story, or break the binding chains of deception that had landed any of us into our mortal stupor. There was no journey I could travel—except my own. I realized that if the Lord took me that moment, I would leave every person I had encountered, my husband, my children, even the people in the ministry—in the hands of Jesus. He owned it all. Everyone and everything belonged to Him.

It was at that moment that I released every burden and care I had carried into that hospital. The years, the people, the anguish—I opened my hands, my heart, my mind, and I let it all go. I released it all, the women, those broken families, and every unending court case. Even my own children—all were in the hands of Jesus. That's where they belonged all along. What had caused me turmoil in the night watches, became a simple prayer, and I went to sleep.

Emerging from that experience, I learned to value being in the moment with the people God places there. People come, and people go. Some succeed, and some do not. There will be individuals who embrace holiness and transformation, but even more who will refuse to change. I had to reckon with the truth that if God's love didn't motivate people to change, mine certainly would not! But just as God extends His unconditional love to us all—I determined to offer the same, without respect of persons! People bound by the lust of their flesh always seem to gravitate toward each other, confined to having only a "form of godliness." It is hard to watch, but undeniably in the Word of God! There are, however, people who gladly receive all the Lord offers, becoming washed by water and the Word and do whatever the Lord requires. They change!

I realized that many reject the Lord's invitation. Still, there will be many, whom I have yet to meet, who will receive Him and remain as clay in the Potter's hands, examining themselves, mortifying their flesh, crucified with Christ. God called me to serve them both, and I will pray for God to make His purpose glorious in all of us who seek to please Him. The Father desires to see every daughter lose the characteristics of Eve: deceptive curiosity, willfulness, and carnal mindedness, that she might gain the posture of submission to the Master. Ready to change. Ready to grow, prepared for reconciliation, forgiving, and being forgiven. That she might once again live in that place of peaceful perfection God intended, as a beautiful daughter of the Most High. Holy. Pure. Unspotted by the world. Not easily influenced. She must know that she has a true Father who will never leave her, even if her natural father did. That daughter will learn that God loves her and has fully equipped her to flourish in the talents and gifts she alone possesses. She can overcome old ways, carnal thoughts, and former influences that separate her from the Father. And she can grow in the rays of Christ's sunlight, prospering in His hand. God willing, I will continue to strive to be ever faithful to my purpose: to be a well-spring and conduit of reconciliation to all who seek Him. I truly desire to prosper the Kingdom and finish my course hearing God say, "Well done thou good and faithful servant."

Pearls From Portia's Story:

o **Listening to the wrong voice can change your life and legacy.**

o **Only God's divine intervention can uncover and break the stronghold of deception.**

o **Whatever or whomever we put before God becomes our god!**

o **All souls belong to God.**

o **Finish your course!**

The Greatest Reconciliation Story

This work tells of nine women who courageously pursued lost relationships. Each of them enacted a plan to reconcile with people who brought meaning to their lives. To do this, they considered these tough questions:

- "Was the relationship worth saving?"
- "Could they mend the breach?"
- "Would recovering the relationship add to or diminish their quality of life?"
- "Were they willing to do anything necessary to fix the relationship?"
- "If rejected, how would they handle it?"

These women worked hard to push past pride, pain, shame, and guilt, maintaining one focus—reconciliation.

Yet as meaningful and powerful as this reconciliation journey has been, there is one story that surpasses them all—the story of humankind becoming reconciled to God. Spiritual reconciliation is the greatest reconciliation story ever told! In this story, we find the fallen, frail, and sinful state of man, amid the unconditional, immeasurable, and atoning love of God. In one sacrificial act, God surrendered the one thing He loved so dearly to restore His kinship and relationship with humankind—He gave His only begotten son.

145

God is our maker, the author, and finisher of our faith. He is the Lord. The creator of the ends of the earth! By His own confession we learn that God made us for His glory: *"Even every one that is called by my name: for I have created him for my glory, I have formed him; yea, I have made him" (Isaiah 43:7).* Our relationship, our kinship, and our connection with God are most important. Yet from the very first man formed to every soul born today, we find ourselves in perpetual discord and enmity with our God. Why? Because of the deadly consequences of a tiny three-letter word—SIN! The day Adam disobeyed God in the Garden of Eden, sin became a damning thread in every human's moral genome. From that day forward, everyone would be *"born in sin and shapen in iniquity"* (Psalm 51:5). When Adam disobeyed God, he hid himself, and God cried out, *"Adam...where art thou?"* (Genesis 3:9) And He is still calling today: *"(Your Name)... Where art thou?"* Some have answered. But many have not. Have you?

The Breach

The book of Genesis is the very first book of the Holy Bible. It tells of Earth's creation and man's first days of life. Unfortunately, these opening pages also chronicle how soon man fell into sin in this utopian paradise God built for him. As early as Genesis 6:5 man's wickedness was *"great in the earth."* The downward spiral began in Genesis 3:1, when they met the serpent. By the end of that chapter Eve was deceived, Adam disobeyed, and God exacted punishment for their misconduct. The corruption the fallen angel exacted upon man caused the

146

whole earth to suffer. In just six brief chapters, the perfect and glorious became perverse and polluted.

The first chapters provide a graphic depiction of God's caring handiwork in the creation. Plant life—God created it. Birds, fishes, cattle, and creeping things—God created them all, yet not one of these was created in God's own image. But the man was! The first man, Adam, was formed from the dust of the earth and made in the very image of God. Then the woman, Eve, was formed from Adam's rib.

How Our Story Began:

Genesis 1:1
"In the beginning, God created the heaven and the earth."

Genesis 2:7
"And the Lord God formed man of the dust of the ground, and breathed into his nostrils the breath of life: and man became a living soul."

Genesis 2:9
"And out of the ground made the Lord God to grow every tree that is pleasant to the sight, and good for food; the tree of life also in the midst of the garden, and the tree of knowledge of good and evil."

Genesis 2:15-17
"And the Lord God took the man, and put him into the garden of Eden to dress it and to keep it. And the Lord God commanded the man, saying, of every tree of the garden thou

mayest freely eat: But of the tree of the knowledge of good and evil, thou shalt not eat of it: for in the day that thou eatest thereof thou shalt surely die."

Genesis 2:18, 21-25

"And the Lord God said, It is not good that the man should be alone; I will make him an help meet for him. And the Lord God caused a deep sleep to fall upon Adam, and he slept: and he took one of his ribs, and closed up the flesh instead thereof; And the rib, which the Lord God had taken from man, made he a woman, and brought her unto the man. And Adam said, This is now bone of my bones, and flesh of my flesh: she shall be called Woman, because she was taken out of Man. Therefore shall a man leave his father and his mother, and shall cleave unto his wife: and they shall be one flesh. And they were both naked, the man and his wife, and were not ashamed."

The Genesis account provides critical knowledge that is irrefutable: God created the world in six days. The seventh day He ordained as His day of rest. Then He formed man from dust, organic matter that He also made! God breathed life into man, and gave the man a job, with specific instructions: (1) dress the garden; and (2) do not eat of The Tree of the Knowledge of Good and Evil. If Adam followed these instructions, God promised success and abundant life! There was Adam; he had a relationship, responsibility, and purpose. And God saw that the man was alone. So, He put Adam to sleep, took a rib, and made him a woman. Eve took her first breath and opened her eyes to a new life, complete with a husband and God's established order. God called "their name" Adam (this explains why a woman takes her husband's name when she marries), and gave them free rein in the Garden. There was one exception: the Tree of the Knowledge of Good and Evil—it was off limits! Now it's interesting to note that this tree is mentioned in Genesis 2:9 along with another very important tree—the Tree of Life! Both trees were in the midst of the garden, yet only one was off-limits—The Tree of the Knowledge of Good and Evil! That's right, Adam could have eaten fruit from the Tree of Life, which would have made man immortal! (Genesis 3:22) And had he done that, the search for the fountain of youth would be non-existent to this day. Neither would we have the unending temptation of tasting "forbidden fruit!" It all started in the garden: wanting what you can't have, what's off-limits!

Where Our Story Shifted:
Something was stirring in Eden, and it's the stuff that makes riveting novels, and multi-million-dollar movies. There was trouble in paradise. Seem like an oxymoron? It was! There was a secret enemy whose intention was to disrupt, discombobulate, even destroy God's glorious and pure creation, to transform paradise into perdition. In walked evil, dressed in a slithering opulent disguise. With him came lies, jealousy, deception, temptation, and yes, death! Along came the fallen angel, the subtle serpent Lucifer—who in Heaven, sought to lift himself above the most high, until God thwarted his plan, dismantling the coup. God cast Lucifer, and his evil recruits out of heaven forever.

149

Revelation 12:7-9
"And there was war in heaven: Michael and his angels fought against the dragon; and the dragon fought and his angels, And prevailed not; neither was their place found any more in heaven. And the great dragon was cast out, that old serpent, called the Devil, and Satan, which deceiveth the whole world: he was cast out into the earth, and his angels were cast out with him."

These verses tell how God cast him out of Heaven and into the earth, where he proceeded to deceive the "whole world." This event in history revealed three undeniable truths:

(1) Both good and evil are real!

(2) Activity in spiritual realms affects the earth and its inhabitants!

(3) The world is in a deceived state because of Satan's evil.

The prophets Isaiah and Ezekiel wrote about Satan, his first estate, and the inevitable consequences God exacted upon him for his sin, deception, and ultimate revolt:

Isaiah 14:12-17
"How art thou fallen from heaven, O Lucifer, son of the morning! how art thou cut down to the ground, which didst weaken the nations! For thou hast said in thine heart, I will ascend into heaven, I will exalt my throne above the stars of God: I will sit also upon the mount of the congregation, in the sides of the north: I will ascend above the heights of the clouds; I will be like the most High. Yet thou shalt be brought down to

150

hell, to the sides of the pit. They that see thee shall narrowly look upon thee, and consider thee, saying, Is this the man that made the earth to tremble, that did shake kingdoms; That made the world as a wilderness, and destroyed the cities thereof; that opened not the house of his prisoners?"

Ezekiel 28:13-19

"Thou hast been in Eden the garden of God; every precious stone was thy covering, the sardius, topaz, and the diamond, the beryl, the onyx, and the jasper, the sapphire, the emerald, and the carbuncle, and gold: the workmanship of thy tabrets and of thy pipes was prepared in thee in the day that thou wast created. Thou art the anointed cherub that covereth; and I have set thee so: thou wast upon the holy mountain of God; thou hast walked up and down in the midst of the stones of fire. Thou wast perfect in thy ways from the day that thou wast created, till iniquity was found in thee. By the multitude of thy merchandise they have filled the midst of thee with violence, and thou hast sinned: therefore I will cast thee as profane out of the mountain of God: and I will destroy thee, O covering cherub, from the midst of the stones of fire. Thine heart was lifted up because of thy beauty, thou hast corrupted thy wisdom by reason of thy brightness: I will cast thee to the ground, I will lay thee before kings, that they may behold thee. Thou hast defiled thy sanctuaries by the multitude of thine iniquities, by the iniquity of thy traffick; therefore will I bring forth a fire from the midst of thee, it shall devour thee, and I will bring thee to ashes upon the earth in the sight of all them that behold thee.

*All they that know thee among the people shall be astonished
at thee: thou shalt be a terror, and never shalt thou be any
more."*

Jude 1:6
*"And the angels which kept not their first estate, but left their
own habitation, he hath reserved in everlasting chains under
darkness unto the judgment of the great day."*

Revelation 12:4
*"And his tail drew the third part of the stars of heaven, and
did cast them to the earth: and the dragon stood before the
woman which was ready to be delivered, for to devour her child
as soon as it was born."*

These verses describe Lucifer, his influence, and
aspiration to exalt his throne above the stars of God!
Because he allowed his beauty to corrupt him, he became
the embodiment of evil. God purged Heaven by casting
him out, along with every angel under his evil influence.
Revelation 20 describes their role and judgment in the last
days—they will be cast into the lake of fire and brimstone
to be tormented forever! However, until his last judgment
occurs, he determines to wreak much devastation and
evil upon God's creation, which is clear in these real-life
events:

❖ **Sin made the world a wilderness**
   The word, wilderness means uncultured, uninhabited,
   and inhospitable. It is empty of pathways, not changed
   by human activity. First words that come to mind when

someone speaks of the wilderness are desert, desolate, and danger. The wilderness is a place of loneliness and barrenness, with no trace of civilization. It is not one's destination but an unexpected, unoccupied, and undesired pitstop. Exodus 14:11 reads: *And they said unto Moses, Because there were no graves in Egypt, hast thou taken us away to die in the wilderness? Wherefore hast thou dealt thus with us, to carry us forth out of Egypt?* The Hebrews thought they would die in the wilderness! According to the prophet Isaiah, it was Lucifer that made the world a wilderness. At creation, it was not so. Genesis 1:11-12 reveals:

"And God said, Let the earth bring forth grass, the herb yielding seed, and the fruit tree yielding fruit after his kind, whose seed is in itself, upon the earth: and it was so. And the earth brought forth grass, and herb yielding seed after his kind, and the tree yielding fruit, whose seed was in itself, after his kind: and God saw that it was good."

There was nothing desolate and inhospitable about the earth when God created it! Genesis 2:9 reveals that the Lord God made "every tree that is pleasant to the sight, and good for food." Genesis 1:29 reads: *And God said, Behold, I have given you every herb bearing seed, which is upon the face of all the earth, and every tree, in the which is the fruit of a tree yielding seed; to you it shall be for meat.* God intended the inhabitants of the earth to live in beauty and with provision for sustenance. But when Our Story changed, so did the Earth!

❖ The start of the End: Sin Manifested in the Earth — Genesis Three

When God created Adam and Eve, He placed them in paradise; the Garden of Eden. Life was perfect, and so was their fellowship with their maker. But while one of God's creations was enjoying the pleasantries of new life, others—Lucifer and the fallen angels had become worse than disgruntled employees. Lucifer determined to exact revenge upon God. But knowing that he could not wage war on God and win, he chose the next best target—the creatures God made for His glory— humankind. He would defile, debase, and defeat them.

Genesis 3:1-7

"Now the serpent was more subtil than any beast of the field which the Lord God had made. And he said unto the woman, Yea, hath God said, Ye shall not eat of every tree of the garden? And the woman said unto the serpent, We may eat of the fruit of the trees of the garden: But of the fruit of the tree which is in the midst of the garden, God hath said, Ye shall not eat of it, neither shall ye touch it, lest ye die. And the serpent said unto the woman, Ye shall not surely die: For God doth know that in the day ye eat thereof, then your eyes shall be opened, and ye shall be as gods, knowing good and evil. And when the woman saw that the tree was good for food, and that it was pleasant to the eyes, and a tree to be desired to make one wise, she took of the fruit thereof, and did eat, and gave also unto her

154

husband with her; and he did eat. And the eyes of them both were opened, and they knew that they were naked; and they sewed fig leaves together, and made themselves aprons."

Let us examine the devices the enemy used:
1) A seed of doubt: "Hath God said…"
2) A half-truth which was a lie: "Ye shall not <u>surely</u> die…"
3) A seed of exaltation: "Ye shall be as gods…"
4) One truth: "…Knowing good and evil…"

James 1:14 reveals something significant:
"But every man is tempted, when he is drawn away of his own lust, and enticed."

Up to this point in the story, there was nothing that indicated Eve questioned her existence, God's instructions or general curiosity about the forbidden tree. But once tempted the desire to taste the forbidden fruit grew into lust. That lust moved Eve to question God's authority, His truthfulness, and even His intentions. Flesh took over quickly. The fruit enticed her, for it looked very appealing—the lust of the eye; she salivated for the delicious novel experience—the lust of the flesh; and she became intrigued by the prospect of becoming as gods, knowing good and evil—the pride of life (1John 2:16).

Being deceived, "She did eat." Then she, "Gave unto her husband with her and he did eat." Adam was

155

right there the whole time. He stood there, idle, while evil courted his wife! Adam was still in charge but he did not take charge. His inaction was a decision: "I will allow it because I'm curious too!"

One bite of the forbidden fruit and everything changed: their eyes became opened, and rather than seeing themselves and the world around them through God's pure, untainted perspective, they saw life through carnal, guilty, shameful eyes. They knew they were naked. Embarrassed before each other and God, they sewed fig leaves to make aprons to cover their nakedness. Both the lie and their sin exposed, they became debased by shame—not exalted as "gods." Another important lesson: Satan is a liar and the father of it (John 8:44). Not once did Lucifer tell them they would know embarrassment, shame, guilt, or estrangement from God—experiences he knew all too well! So, they hid from God. It was at that point that man became not only servants of the wicked one, but they became like him—the one they obeyed.

Romans 6:16
"*Know ye not, that to whom ye yield yourselves servants to obey, his servants ye are to whom ye obey; whether of sin unto death, or of obedience unto righteousness?*"

THE FALL OF MANKIND
Adam and Eve both yielded to their conceived lust rather than resisting temptation to maintain their relationship with their maker. The result: the

156

introduction and reign of sin in all the earth. From that point on, every man would be *"born in sin and shapen in iniquity"* (Psalms 51:5), in the likeness of the one they obeyed — the devil. For this, God pronounced three irrevocable judgments:

#1 Curse Upon the Serpent: Genesis 3:14

"And the Lord God said unto the serpent, Because thou hast done this, thou art cursed above all cattle, and above every beast of the field; upon thy belly shalt thou go, and dust shalt thou eat all the days of thy life."

#2 Curse Upon the Woman: Genesis 3:16

"Unto the woman he said, I will greatly multiply thy sorrow and thy conception; in sorrow thou shalt bring forth children; and thy desire shall be to thy husband, and he shall rule over thee."

#3 Curse Upon the Man: Genesis 3:17-19

"And unto Adam he said, Because thou hast hearkened unto the voice of thy wife, and hast eaten of the tree, of which I commanded thee, saying, Thou shalt not eat of it: cursed is the ground for thy sake; in sorrow shalt thou eat of it all the days of thy life; Thorns also and thistles shall it bring forth to thee; and thou shalt eat the herb of the field; In the sweat of thy face shalt thou eat bread, till thou return unto the ground; for out of it wast thou taken: for dust thou art, and unto dust shalt thou return."

The Evidence of Inherent Sin: Lies and Murder

After God pronounced judgment on Adam and Eve, He "drove out the man" from the Garden of Eden (Genesis 3:24) and positioned a Cherubim and flaming sword "to keep the tree of life." Because Adam and Eve knew good and evil, they forfeited their intended inheritance—immortality. The consequences of that choice became clear as they started their family.

"And Adam knew Eve his wife; and she conceived, and bare Cain, and said, I have gotten a man from the Lord." (Genesis 4:1) Then Eve bore another son, Abel. *The Bible says, "And in the process of time…"* the boys brought offerings to God—Cain brought of the fruit of the ground, and Abel of the firstlings of his flock (Genesis 4:3-4). But when God had respect for Abel's offering, Cain became "very wroth." Cain's disdain and fallen countenance caused God to talk with him, identifying that his attitude revealed sin (Genesis 4:5-7). Yet rather than dealing with his own sinful heart, Cain engaged his brother in a conversation that left Abel dead, for Cain killed Abel. When God inquired, *"Where is Abel, thy brother?"* Cain's reply was both untrue and irreverent: *"I know not: Am I my brother's keeper?" (Genesis 4:9)* God knew the answer, but Cain needed to face his sin and the immoral crime that ensued from it. He needed to own the truth and answer for his crime. As much as people deny it, even today, man is accountable to God, our maker.

Cain was in a fallen state that produced jealousy, pride, and hatred. He had become a deceitful liar who was insolent, insubordinate, and defiant. His sin led to violence and murder! This lengthy list reveals how sin, unchecked, affects everything! Communion with God, familial relationships, order, humanity, and even our environment—sin can cause us to risk it all.

The downward spiral continued. In Genesis Six, the man had become so wicked before God, marrying every fair maid they chose, that God reacted:

(1) God said He would not always strive with man.
(2) God reduced man's life to 120 years.
(3) God repented that He had made man for His heart grieved.
(4) God determined to destroy man.

❀ **The End and a New Beginning: The Flood—Genesis Six**

From childhood, the impression given was that Noah preached, "It's going to rain! Get in the ark!" But the actual account in Genesis reveals something different. There was no preaching or words of warning to the sinful inhabitants of the earth—no rejection or ridiculing Noah that's documented in the Word. Man's corrupt state had become so aberrant that God determined to begin again with one family—Noah's:

159

Genesis 6:12-13, 17-18

"And God looked upon the earth, and, behold, it was corrupt; for all flesh had corrupted his way upon the earth. And God said unto Noah, The end of all flesh is come before me; for the earth is filled with violence through them; and, behold, I will destroy them with the earth. And, behold, I, even I, do bring a flood of waters upon the earth, to destroy all flesh, wherein is the breath of life, from under heaven; and every thing that is in the earth shall die. But with thee will I establish my covenant; and thou shalt come into the ark, thou, and thy sons, and thy wife, and thy sons' wives with thee."

Because God witnessed righteousness in Noah, He made an exclusive invitation for sanctuary from the impending doom that would come upon the whole earth (Genesis 7:1). Noah and his family were the only humans invited into the ark, along with fowls, cattle, and creeping things (Genesis 6:20). With these, God would replenish the earth following the flood. He would begin again.

What's so interesting about the Genesis account is that it disproves the common belief that, "Everybody can't be wrong!" In Noah's day, almost everyone certainly was! The majority was wrong and sinful, and thus, destroyed.

♦ **Sin Resumes After the Flood: Genesis 9—10**
NOAH'S SONS: SHEM, HAM, AND JAPHETH

In Genesis nine, when Noah's family emerged from the ark, Noah became an husbandmen, which means planter or farmer. He planted a vineyard. When he drank of the wine produced by his grapes, he got drunk. His son Ham, the father of Canaan, *"saw the nakedness of his father"* (Genesis 9:22-23) and told his two brothers, Shem and Japheth who honored their father by covering him and walking out backwards, refusing to look upon him. For this, Noah honored Shem and Japheth. But because of Ham's disrespect, Noah pronounced a curse on Ham's son Canaan; he would serve Shem and Japheth.

THE CURSE ON HAM CONTINUES:
Nimrod and the Tower of Babel

Ham's son, Nimrod, became the king of Babel. We simply define babel as "A confused noise made by many voices." But what Nimrod's story reveals is the true origin of the word; Babel was an actual place! It was here that Nimrod enacted a vision so powerful that even God came down to behold the unity it evoked in the people. God's revelatory statement: *"Behold, the people is one, and they have all one language; and this they begin to do: and now nothing will be restrained from them, which they have imagined to do" (Genesis 11:6).* God's instruction to the souls who emerged from the ark was to go forth and replenish the earth. Nimrod, however, determined to do the opposite:

Genesis 11:1-4

"And the whole earth was of one language, and of one speech...And they said, Go to, let us build us a city and a tower whose top may reach unto heaven; and let us make us a name, lest we be scattered abroad upon the face of the whole earth."

Once again, evil forces got the best of even this second generation of humankind, proving that the very nature of man was perpetually sinful. What was so wrong with building the city and erecting a tower? (1) Nimrod was disobedient; instead of following God's instruction, he made his own decision—build a city and a tower to reach heaven! (2) Nimrod was prideful. His desire, "Let us make us a name!" God's remedy in Genesis 11:7 is a powerful revelation of the origin of Babel: *"Go to, let us go down, and there confound their language, that they may not understand one another's speech."* Babel would not become a glorious city with an impressive ascending tower, but nothing more than an infamous state of confusion with Nimrod exacting his father's disobedient and prideful legacy! No longer able to comprehend each other's speech, they scattered and unwillingly fulfilled God's instructions to replenish the earth.

❖ Sodom and Gomorrah: The Destruction of Two Cities

Genesis 19 recounts Sodom and Gomorrah, two cities destroyed because of sin. The particular sin that prevailed in these two towns is becoming more widespread in today's culture. This generation is so inundated with "tolerance" that even the Christian community fails to herald the truth found in God's Word:

Jude 1:7-8

"Even as Sodom and Gomorrha, and the cities about them in like manner, giving themselves over to fornication, and going after strange flesh, are set forth for an example, suffering the vengeance of eternal fire. Likewise also these filthy dreamers defile the flesh, despise dominion, and speak evil of dignities."

Leviticus 18:22

"Thou shalt not lie with mankind, as with womankind: it is abomination."

Romans 1:26-28

"For this cause God gave them up unto vile affections: for even their women did change the natural use into that which is against nature: and likewise also the men, leaving the natural use of the woman, burned in their lust one toward another; men with men working that which is unseemly, and receiving in themselves that recompense of their error which was meet. And even as they did not like to retain God in their knowledge, God gave them over to a

reprobate mind, to do those things which are not convenient."

Both the Old and New Testaments identify the reason that God destroyed Sodom and Gomorrha was sexual sin, both fornication and engaging with "strange flesh," which in today's vernacular is homosexuality. Though some argue that the actual problem was more about hospitality, others pin the phrase on the men's desire for angelic beings. However, this account is explicit that the angels appeared in the form of regular men. The Sodomites surrounded the house, demanding for Lot to give them the men who entered his house. *"I pray, brethren, do not so wickedly. Behold now, I have two daughters which have not known man; let me, I pray you, bring them out unto you, and do ye to them as is good in your eyes: only unto these men do nothing" (Genesis 19:7-8).* These verses clarify that the Sodomites had sexual intentions, which Lot identified as wicked, suggesting that they instead "do ye to them" (meaning his daughters) what they intended to "do to" the men. Leviticus 18:22 makes God's instructions clear: *"Thou shalt not lie with mankind, as with womankind: it is abomination."* The word abomination means a thing that causes disgust or hatred; disgrace, obscenity, evil, crime. Thus the term, sodomy, which means: sexual intercourse involving anal or oral copulation. In Romans 1:26-28, Paul identifies such behavior as "vile affections," he uses the words, unseemly, error, reprobate, and "not convenient."

164

In the United States, sodomy remained illegal until 2003, which in the scheme of historical timelines, is thousands of years after God revealed His laws for moral living. Why is this important? Sodomy has been deemed immoral, criminal, and contrary to God's laws for moral living even through modern times. There is a new "normal" that labels those who follow God's laws as judgmental or intolerant. And thus the paradigm for morality is shifting. Anyone who pushes back against this shifted perspective is accused of discrimination or instilling hate. God's Word is clear.

2 Timothy 3:1-13 forewarns us of the condition of the last days: *"perilous times shall come."* Explaining that, *"Evil men and seducers shall wax worse and worse."* Knowledge has exponentially increased in just the last 100 years, so morality has exponentially decreased in the same period.

❖ Souls are captive
2 Timothy 2:24-26

"And the servant of the Lord must not strive; but be gentle unto all men, apt to teach, patient, In meekness instructing those that oppose themselves; if God peradventure will give them repentance to the acknowledging of the truth; And that they may recover themselves out of the snare of the devil, who are taken captive by him at his will."

The devil has set a snare for us! And according to this verse, many are taken captive at **his will**—according to **his plan!** The problem is that many people don't know Satan has captured them. Why? Because Satan's traps often come in the form of something familiar, something desirable, and something popular. The pitfalls of these traps include subtle destructive habits like overeating, laziness, and procrastination. They include fleshly desires like sexual lust, gambling, or drugs. Satan's strongholds also come in the form of social, political, religious, and even moral views adopted from celebrity icons; from excessive spending to keep up with popular trends; from doing things that get "likes" or approval on social media. Just look at what God's word says about these traps:

1 Corinthians 6:9-10

"Know ye not that the unrighteous shall not inherit the kingdom of God? Be not deceived: neither fornicators, nor idolaters, nor adulterers, nor effeminate, nor abusers of themselves with mankind, Nor thieves, nor covetous, nor drunkards, nor revilers, nor extortioners, shall inherit the kingdom of God."

Luke 21:34

"And take heed to yourselves, lest at any time your hearts be overcharged with surfeiting, and drunkenness, and cares of this life, and so that day come upon you unawares."

John 12:43

"For they loved the praise of men more than the praise of God."

Seven Things God Hates: Proverbs 6:16-19

These six things doth the Lord Hate: yea, seven are an abomination unto him: 1. A proud look 2. A lying tongue 3. Hands that shed innocent blood 4. An heart that devises wicked imaginations 5. Feet that be swift in running to mischief 6. A false witness that speaks lies 7. Sewing discord among brethren.

Many souls are captive to these seven abominations—a big word, rarely mentioned these days. It means: something that causes disgust or hatred. God loathes these seven abominations, therefore we should seek to share His same view. Yet engaging in them has become a normal and expected part of everyday life. It's common to hear the phrase, "I'm so proud of you!" We make excuses for telling "white lies." Innocent lives are taken everyday—including unborn babies by the millions. Men make wicked devices, murderous video games, mutilating inventions, drug paraphernalia, sex toys. People go out of their way to get into trouble, engaging others to join them. They lie, cheat, and steal from the elderly, hard-working citizens, and children. And people think nothing of separating friends, even if they have to lie to do it!

♦ **The nations are weakened**

War, disease, and poverty are just a few crippling agents. But, the greatest evil man faces is rising immorality. Sin is the cause behind greed, financial scams, assault and murder, sexual misconduct, domestic violence, addictions, and all activities contrived to support these acts, behaviors, and promulgations. It cripples populations all over the world.

♦ **The earth trembles**

Trending News in just the last five years evidenced a rise in earthquakes, hurricanes, tornados, floods, volcanic eruptions, and wildfires—including the United States, Canada, Japan, Greece, and many other regions around the world. There have been so many hurricanes in the year 2020 that the names went into the greek alphabet! Such disasters were not what God intended when He created the Heaven and the Earth. These too are consequences of our fallen state.

♦ **Kingdoms are shaken**

The word shaken means: jolt or shock. When kingdoms are shaken, something has happened that leaves unexpected and widespread alarm and consequences. How are the kingdoms shaken?

Genocide
In the last 100 years there were multiple occurrences of genocide against Jews, Armenians, Cambodians, Bosnians, and citizens of Rwanda and Darfur.

Political Upheaval
The 2017 Brexit caused unrest in Britain/United Kingdom and Northern Ireland when they left the European Union. In the United States, the election of private citizen/billionaire Donald J. Trump was the start of upheaval between Republicans and Democrats that left some spreading rumors of regression to a divided country resembling the pre-civil war era.

Terrorist Attacks
Mainstream headlines of escalating terrorism around the globe are sending shockwaves of unrest, setting new paradigms of the notion of world peace. Citizens are increasingly concerned for their safety. Targets have no particular profile, and perpetrators often have no stated biases. These terrorists use suicide bombers, runaway airplanes, explosive devices, automatic weapons, and even mailed chemical substances. They strike in random patterns and random territories. Whether a super-power, like the United States, or a nation laden with unceasing war and civil unrest, terrorism is a global concern in this century. According to forbes.com, some of the most massive terror activity occurs in the Middle East, Asia, and Africa. However, the United States had a rude awakening on September 11, 2001, as we

watched the twin towers struck by hijacked airplanes. 2,996 souls perished among the ashes, with one of them being my cousin Margaret who called my Aunt Katie to say, "I love you!" Terrorism can touch anyone either directly or indirectly, and at any time without warning.

The Threat of Nuclear War

The Nuclear Arms Race continues as North Korean president, Kim Jong Un proceeds with missile launch tests against cautions from the United Nations and the White House. Militaristic readiness becomes an escalating concern in our country and abroad.

Pestilence: The Coronavirus/Covid-19

The breaking headline for 2020 is the pandemic ravaging nations around the world. Unexpectedly, this virus shook the world as citizens in Wuhan China became mysteriously stricken with such a force that it left world leaders in a quagmire of how to stay its spread. Italy soon followed, with the United States not far behind. As the death toll continued to rise, travel ceased. Business shut down. And the White House and state officials issued a "shelter-in edict" in America. By late March 2020, there were over 566,000 cases across the world, with over 25,000 fatalities, over 1300 ascribed to the United States. Fortunately, more than 129,000 recovered from the illness (worldometers.info). Even as I write this chapter, we continue the shelter-in mandate, hoping the pandemic will cease by the holidays.

Headlines and happenings in the world are the evidence that these are perilous times. As sin escalates, so does the moral depravity of our world. War and violence ravage countries, cities, and communities. The earth and God's creatures suffer environmental disasters. Citizens are alarmed as political systems, governments, and law enforcement collapse. Moral values continue to decline. And the very structure of the family is under attack as gender and marriage, ordained from Earth's creation, are redefined—not by our maker, but by the one whom God made—man. The unborn are sacrificed upon the altar of the pro-choice movement. And men are in constant rebellion of God's rules, seeking rather an humanistic approach that leans toward self-rule. Similar to Judges 17:6, "In those days there was no king in Israel, but every man did that which was right in his own eyes." Simply put, we are seeing the signs of an anarchistic society—a state of disorder due to the absence or nonrecognition of Heavenly and Earthly authority. This world is in trouble, and sin is the culprit behind it all.

Because Adam sinned, the very nature of man became altered. Every person would forever be conceived in sin and *"shapen in iniquity."* Humankind's DNA was transformed from good into corrupt, from moral to immoral, and from eternal to transient. A soul would never enter the world as a good, sinless immortal being as God intended. But every soul would emerge from the womb with a flawed nature, inclined to sin—destined to "surely die."

"And God saw that the wickedness of man was great in the earth, and that every imagination of the thoughts of his heart was only evil continually" (Genesis 6:5). Isaiah 59:2 reads: *"But your iniquities have separated between you and your God, and your sins have hid his face from you, that he will not hear."*

People don't like to think of themselves as sinful, but rather good-hearted, with a natural moral compass that points in the right direction. But the evidence is clear— sometimes that compass fails and even the good-intentioned fall prey to the dark side of their nature. And we can't help it! No wonder Paul penned these troubling but true words in Romans 7:14-24:

"For we know that the law is spiritual: but I am carnal, sold under sin. For that which I do I allow not: for what I would, that do I not; but what I hate, that do I. If then I do that which I would not, I consent unto the law that it is good. Now then it is no more I that do it, but sin that dwelleth in me. For I know that in me (that is, in my flesh,) dwelleth no good thing: for to will is present with me; but how to perform that which is good I find not. For the good that I would I do not: but the evil which I would not, that I do. Now if I do that I would not, it is no more I that do it, but sin that dwelleth in me. I find then a law, that, when I would do good, evil is present with me. For I delight in the law of God after the inward man: But I see another law in my members, warring against the law of my mind, and bringing me into captivity to the law of sin which is in my members. O wretched man that I am! who shall deliver me from the body of this death?"

Sin. Defined it means: crime, offense, wrongdoing, evil. Sin has left us with wicked intents, evil imaginations, and just plain bad behavior. Our badness juxtaposed to God's goodness leads us to only one conclusion—we need help! It's not in us to be good or do good, not without an unction from the One who is innately good. That is God. There is no sin in Him. Mark 10:18 reveals, *"...There is none good but one, that is God."* But the very essence of our being is sinful. And that has separated us from God. *"But your iniquities have separated between you and your God, and your sins have hid his face from you, that he will not hear" (Isaiah 59:2).* Sin offends God and separates us from Him.

In today's culture, even on Christian radio, the word sin is being replaced with words like "shortcomings," "mistakes," or "poor choices." These euphemisms downplay the truth—there is right, and there is wrong. Even when we want to do what's right, our fallen nature pulls us into wrongdoing. And alas we must admit the one truth nobody wants to face: we are prone to wrongdoing. One comedian made a joke of this woeful truth, "The devil made me do it!" And while millions laughed, like Paul, we must admit: *"For the good that I would I do not: but the evil which I would not, that I do!"* (Romans 7:19) Paul concluded by saying, *"O wretched man that I am! Who shall deliver me from the body of this death?"* We sin with our bodies, but the soul will reap the consequences: *"The soul that sinneth, it shall die"*(Ezekiel 18:20), that's the bad news. The good news is that God made a way of escape—the Lord Jesus Christ: *"How shall* we escape, if we neglect so great salvation; which at the first began to be spoken by the Lord, and was confirmed unto us by them that heard him!" (Hebrews 2:3) The Scriptures reveal that Jesus is our salvation: *"For God so loved the world, that he gave his only begotten Son, that whosoever believeth in him should not perish, but have everlasting life. For God sent not his Son into the world to condemn the world; but that the world through him might be saved."* (John 3:16-17) Though we were born in sin, and have become captive to it, God sent His only begotten son to save us from it! Jesus is our Saviour: *"Neither is there salvation in any other: for there is none other name under heaven given among men, whereby we must be saved."* (Acts 4:12) That is the greatest reconciliation story ever told—the restoring of man's relationship with God. After all we have done the perfect, sinless Creator still wants to have a relationship with us! Nothing has discouraged Him from loving or coming after us; disobedience, rejection, murder, deceit, sexual immorality, addiction—not even our crimes against each other. But as a loving Father, He remains kind and charitable to each and every one of us, making a way for us to get life right!

Take a look at these scriptures:

Leviticus 17:11   Old Testament: Introduction of Temporal Atonement
*"For the life of the flesh is in the blood: and I have given it to you upon the altar to make an **atonement** for your souls: for it is the blood that maketh an atonement for the soul."*

174

—The word "atonement" means to remove guilt. Sin is the cause of man's perpetual state of guilt. God introduced a process for atonement or removal of that guilt through a blood sacrifice. The book of Numbers is replete with blood sacrifices to atone for sin, including Numbers 6:14, which describes the lamb offering.

John 1:29 New Testament: Fulfillment of Spiritual/ Everlasting Atonement

"The next day John seeth Jesus coming unto him, and saith, Behold the Lamb of God, which taketh away the sin of the world."
—John the Baptist knew Jesus as the sacrificial lamb who would become the sacrifice for man's sins! Revelation 13:8 identifies Jesus as "The Lamb slain from the foundation of the world."

Romans 5:6-19
"For when we were yet without strength, in due time Christ died for the ungodly.
For scarcely for a righteous man will one die: yet peradventure for a good man some would even dare to die. But God commendeth his love toward us, in that, while we were yet sinners, Christ died for us. Much more then, being now justified by his blood, we shall be saved from wrath through him. For if, when we were enemies, we were reconciled to God by the death of his Son, much more, being reconciled, we shall be saved by his life. And not only so, but we also joy in God through our Lord Jesus Christ, by whom we have now received the atonement. Wherefore, as by one man sin entered into the world, and death by sin; and so death passed upon all men, for that all have sinned: (For until the law sin was in the world:

175

but sin is not imputed when there is no law. Nevertheless death reigned from Adam to Moses, even over them that had not sinned after the similitude of Adam's transgression, who is the figure of him that was to come. But not as the offence, so also is the free gift. For if through the offense of one many be dead, much more the grace of God, and the gift by grace, which is by one man, Jesus Christ, hath abounded unto many. And not as it was by one that sinned, so is the gift: for the judgment was by one to condemnation, but the free gift is of many offences unto justification. For if by one man's offence death reigned by one; much more they which receive abundance of grace and of the gift of righteousness shall reign in life by one, Jesus Christ.) Therefore as by the offence of one judgment came upon all men to condemnation; even so by the righteousness of one the free gift came upon all men unto justification of life. For as by one man's disobedience many were made sinners, so by the obedience of one shall many be made righteous."

The sin (disobedience) of one man, Adam, caused all men to be born in sin. But the righteousness (obedience) of one man, Jesus Christ, enables all men to be born again!

1 Peter 2:21-25
"For even hereunto were ye called: because Christ also suffered for us, leaving us an example, that ye should follow his steps: Who did no sin, neither was guile found in his mouth: Who, when he was reviled, reviled not again; when he suffered, he threatened not; but committed himself to him that judgeth righteously: Who his own self bare our sins in his own body on the tree, that we, being dead to sins, should live unto

righteousness: by whose stripes ye were healed. For ye were as sheep going astray; but are now returned unto the Shepherd and Bishop of your souls."

Jesus Christ, who was pure and sinless, became the sacrifice for the sins of the whole world, bearing man's sins in His own body.

Hebrews 10:1-12
*"For the law having a shadow of good things to come, and not the very image of the things, can never with those sacrifices which they offered year by year continually make the comers thereunto perfect. For then would they not have ceased to be offered? because that the worshippers once purged should have had no more conscience of sins. But in those sacrifices there is a remembrance again made of sins every year. For it is not possible that the blood of bulls and of goats should take away sins. Wherefore when he cometh into the world, he saith, Sacrifice and offering thou wouldest not, but a body hast thou prepared me: In burnt offerings and sacrifices for sin thou hast had no pleasure. Then said I, Lo, I come (in the volume of the book it is written of me,) to do thy will, O God. Above when he said, Sacrifice and offering and burnt offerings and offering for sin thou wouldest not, neither hadst pleasure therein; which are offered by the law; Then said he, Lo, I come to do thy will, O God. He taketh away the first, that he may establish the second. **By the which will we are sanctified through the offering of the body of Jesus Christ once for all. And every priest standeth daily ministering and offering oftentimes the same sacrifices, which can never take away sins: But this man, after he***

had offered one sacrifice for sins for ever, sat down on the right hand of God."

The Old Testament animal sacrifice was a temporary solution to atone for sin. It was required yearly. But when Jesus became sin for us, He became the sacrificial lamb, atoning for sin for all humanity once and for all!

2 Corinthians 5:19
*"To wit, that **God was in Christ**, reconciling the world unto himself, not imputing their trespasses unto them; and hath committed unto us the word of reconciliation."*

Truly Jesus' words on the Cross, "It is finished," irrefutably proclaimed God's completed work of salvation! He finished His work. Now He is looking for our response.

John 1:12
"But as many as received him, to them gave he power to become the sons of God, even to them that believe on his name."

Conclusion

Reconciliation is the focus of this entire work. Why? Because reconciliation is critical and essential to every human being. Though women told the stories contained in this book, don't be fooled—men need to mend broken relationships too! 1 John 4:20 reveals: *"If a man say, I love God, and hateth his brother, he is a liar: for he that loveth not his brother whom he hath seen, how can he love God whom he hath not seen?"* According to God's Word, we are to maintain our relationships with one another—our brothers and sisters that we see in this life every day! It is in that spirit of fellowship that the door becomes open to reconcile with Him! God is saying, *"Love one another, then you can love me! Address your offenses toward each other and then address your offenses toward me!"* Reconciliation is both relevant and urgent! It is so critical that God gave His life for it! All we have to do to honor His sacrifice is (1) reconcile to one another, and (2) receive His great salvation that we might become reconciled to Him. The work to reconcile with the people in your life is up to you. The work to reconcile your soul to God was completed by Jesus Christ on Calvary's cross—all you have to do is receive Him. There are seven essential steps:

1. FAITH
"And they said, Believe on the Lord Jesus Christ, and thou shalt be saved, and thy house." (Acts 16:31)

2. CONFESSION
"That if thou shalt confess with thy mouth the Lord Jesus, and shalt believe in thine heart that God hath raised him from the dead, thou shalt be saved." (Romans 10:9)

3. REPENTANCE
"The Lord is not slack concerning his promise, as some men count slackness; but is longsuffering to us-ward, not willing that any should perish, but that all should come to repentance." (2 Peter 3:9)

4. WATER BAPTISM
"He that believeth and is baptized shall be saved; but he that believeth not shall be damned." (Mark 16:16)

"Then Peter said unto them, Repent, and be baptized every one of you in the name of Jesus Christ for the remission of sins, and ye shall receive the gift of the Holy Ghost." (Acts 2:38)

5. HOLY GHOST
"But ye are not in the flesh, but in the Spirit, if so be that the Spirit of God dwell in you. Now if any man have not the Spirit of Christ, he is none of his." (Romans 8:9)

6. HOLINESS
"Follow peace with all men, and holiness, without which no man shall see the Lord." (Hebrews 12:14)

7. ENDURANCE

"And ye shall be hated of all men for my name's sake: but he that shall endure unto the end, the same shall be saved."
(Mark 13:13)

(Reference: "The 7—Key Steps of Salvation," Joseph R. Hewitt, pastor of Reconciliation Word Ministry Int'l, Royal Oak, MI)

Now I commission you—create your reconciliation story!
Love one another, and Be ye reconciled to God!

Amen.

Acknowledgements

I always felt in my heart that my purpose in life included writing a book. The time just never seemed right, nor could I zero in on any particular topic. But when I returned to college, determined to finally get my degree before I turned 50, everything became clearer. I developed a passion for all things "Family Life!" The puzzle pieces came together. My husband encouraged me. My children pushed me. And I felt that everyone in my circle cheered me on! I am so thankful for this opportunity to share what I've learned.

This book is part anthology, part inspiration, and part instruction. All three parts have required me to engage in dialogue, introspection, study, and prayer. I thank God for leading me and holding my hand from inception through completion. It is with this gratitude that I offer these words of encouragement to you:

Your Family Matters! They are your gift. Love your spouse and each child right where they are. When things go wrong—do all you can to make it right.

Your Friendships Matter! Thomas Aquinas once said, "There is nothing on this earth more to be prized than true friendship." I appreciate the friends in my life who know me well and love me anyway! Give your friends the benefit of the doubt. Listen to them. Learn from them. Love them unconditionally. Forgive them.

God Matters! He shed His blood to not only reconcile us back to Himself—but to give us power to live for Him! He loves you. You were created for His glory. The proof: God created you in His own image, and He has graven you upon the palms of His hands! (Isaiah 49:16) There is nothing too egregious for God's grace. Repent and He will forgive you. I am living proof!

Book—

Love like that

1-800-20L 5200

Relationship secrets

Love stimulates love

Made in the USA
Monee, IL
26 January 2021

58623442R00115